THE FRESHMAN 15

GUIDE TO THRIVE FOR COLLEGE FRESHMEN

KATE HENDERSON

D1710201

CONTENTS

INTRO—DUCTION

Don't you love looking back at old journals and diaries? I have a shelf full of them from third grade to the present. I love flipping through them and seeing the way my handwriting has changed from simple, childlike print to a more girly cursive. I chuckle over the drama that filled the pages from my junior high journals, and I love the precious innocence of those elementary years when my biggest concern was figuring out why the boy I liked pushed me at recess!

My diaries have since become prayer journals. Pen and paper help me pour my heart out to God and talk to Him about all that is going on with me. My prayer journals are an amazing testimony of the incredible ways God has worked in my life. Instead of the innocence and ease of my elementary diaries, the prayer journals are filled with great pain, amazing triumphs and the search for God's will in it all. I love the way that my eyes fill with tears when I read those prayers and remember what an amazing work God was doing in me.

I thought of my journals when I started preparing for this study. I pulled out the ones from my senior year in high school and my freshman year in college. As I read the prayers that I penned so many years ago, all the feelings that accompanied them came flooding back. It was so easy for me to recall my tumultuous and hectic senior year. It was as if the Lord allowed me to travel back in time and take on all that I felt once again. As my eyes scanned the pages I could feel my pulse quicken, my heart pound in my chest and my palms get sweaty. The excitement, anticipation, anxiety and stress of all that I was experiencing at the time I wrote those journal entries came flooding over me.

Reading those journals reminded me of the first day in my senior English class when my teacher told us we were going to *immediately* begin working on the essays that we would send in with our college applications. I remember being shocked and thinking, "It's only August. Don't I have all year to worry about that?" Evidently I didn't. Not only did my teacher seem aware of the rush but so did many of my classmates who had already finished filling out most of their college applications! From that moment on, I knew I had to get on the ball, and I soon discovered that college applications were just the beginning. The madness and whirlwind of my senior year didn't settle down until days after I stepped across the stage to receive my high school diploma.

I bring this up not to make you feel any more anxious than you may already, but just to let you know that I remember. Oh, do I remember! I am so thankful that I had those journals and that the Lord allowed those memories and feelings to wash over me because it immediately made me think of all of you. It strengthened my desire to pour into you and pour God's word over you -- to help give you peace and prepare you for the amazing time of your life that is COLLEGE!

What are you looking forward to about college?

1.

2.

3.

What are you worried or fearful about concerning college?

1.

2.

3.

Don't be deceived by the title, the focus of this study is not the infamous fifteen pounds that seem to haunt freshman girls. No! This is a whole different kind of Freshman 15, and the only kind you need to be concerned about.

The purpose of this study is to prepare you for this great adventure, this segment of your life that you will forever refer to as your "College Years". I believe that the Lord has called me to help pack some helps in your college-bound suitcase so that instead of just surviving, you would thrive during your freshman year and throughout the rest of your college experience. More than anything, I desire that you would grow increasingly closer to the Lord and know Him more deeply as you trust Him to be your Guide through this wild ride!

This study is separated into five chapters that cover topics that are significant to you as a college freshman. They are: Keeping the Faith, Time Management, Dudes and Dating, Your Temple and People and Prayer.

In preparing to leave for college, you will likely make a long list of all of the things you need to pack and then try with all of your might to cram them into your suitcases. I want to make sure that you don't forget to pack 15 very important items. These 15 items will be our "must-packs" that make up The Freshman 15. You will find these must-packs divided into each of the five chapters of the study.

By the end of the study, your college-bound suitcase will be filled with the 15 must-packs that will help you thrive in college. Let's start packing!

KEEPING THE FAITH

Here it comes. Can you see it off in the distance? It's the finish line. You've almost made it. Before too long it will be your turn to walk across that graduation stage and receive your diploma. Can't you just picture it? There you are; all decked out in that snazzy black robe and all-too-stylish graduation cap. Your time has come. And as you walk across the stage and past the finish line, you receive your reward: a diploma and a sense of great accomplishment.

But, wait a minute, what is that looming in the distance beyond the stage? Is that college? Sure enough. A new race will begin soon with new challenges, new adventures and new people. Do you feel a little nervous about this scenario—crossing the finish line of high school knowing that a new race called college is waiting to start?

I was really excited about finishing high school but getting ready to go off to college was stressful. All of the uncertainties about my future made me anxious. Besides trying to figure out which school to go to, how to pay for tuition, what dorm to stay in and what major and classes to choose, I was also worried about how I would hang onto my faith. I had seen so many of my friends go off to school and stray away from the Lord. I wanted to make sure that I grew closer to Him during my college years instead of falling away.

Is this fear one of yours too? I want to prepare you so that you know how to keep your faith in college as I learned to keep mine. I could sugarcoat it, but instead I want to be real with you and warn you that your faith will be tested and challenged during your college years in ways that you probably didn't experience in high school. Some of that testing will come in ways you expect. You may expect to be challenged on what you believe by those who think they have it all figured out and think you don't. You may expect to be ridiculed for taking a stand for Christ. You may expect secular professors to tell you that your religion is a joke and to seek their way of freethinking. You may expect to be pressured into going to parties and "experimenting" with substances at those parties. We've all been warned against these scenarios.

What you may not have been warned against is a testing of your faith that happens so inconspicuously that you don't realize you've lost it until it's already gone. How does this happen? One decision at a time. You get busy. You meet new friends. Suddenly, you're too tired to go to church and there is no one there to make you go. You've been sacrificing your time with the Lord to get more sleep or hang out with your new buddies. Then, little by little, your convictions are eroded. Your passion fades and your faith is gone. Am I sounding a little harsh? If so, it's only because I have seen it happen so many times and I want better for you. I want you to grow exponentially in your faith during your college years. I want your story to be different than the one I just described. I want you to cling to your faith—to keep it. In all honesty, if you don't cling to the Lord, chances are you will cling to something or someone else. Trust me. I've been around long enough to know that clinging to anything other than God always ends in utter disappointment. *Someone* or *something* is not qualified to provide you with all that you need to make it. God has something even better to offer. Instead of just making it, He wants to show you how to THRIVE in college. As a new campus, a new home, new friends, classes, stressors and increased responsibility are heaped on your shoulders, turn to the Lord. It will be your faith in Him that will act as the anchor for your soul and keep you steadfast.

Before you're even an "official" college freshman, your faith is challenged by feelings of anxiety and worry about what's to come. As we discussed in the introduction, there are so many things that make us feel worried or anxious about the future. The Enemy wants to use those anxieties to get us off course. He wants to get us so worked up that we stop seeking Jesus and start trying to figure out how to do everything on our own.

I want you to keep your faith. I want you to put your worries, concerns, time, friends, classes and all the things that will come with your freshman year in the Lord's hands. We do that by learning the first of our 15 must-packs.

We are going to put first things first. So what *must* come first? To remove these anxieties and to really help you thrive, you MUST be in the presence of the Lord. Well intentioned people will try to give you all sorts of tips and advice to help you quell your anticipatory worries, but nothing will provide lasting peace and security except the Lord—knowing Him intimately and allowing Him to rule.

Please read the passage from Matthew 6:25-34:

> Therefore I tell you, do not worry about your life, what you will eat or drink; or about your body, what you will wear. Is not life more important than food, and the body more important than clothes? Look at the birds of the air; they do not sow or reap or store away in barns, and yet your heavenly Father feeds them. Are you not much more valuable than they? Who of you by worrying can add a single hour to his life?

> And why do you worry about clothes? See how the lilies of the field grow. They do not labor or spin. Yet I tell you that not even Solomon in all his splendor was dressed like one of these. If that is how God clothes the grass of the field, which is here today and tomorrow is thrown into the fire, will he not much more clothe you, O you of little faith? So do not worry, saying, 'What shall we eat?' or 'What shall we drink?' or 'What shall we wear?' For the pagans run after all these things, and your heavenly Father knows that you need them. But seek first his kingdom and his righteousness, and all these things will be given to you as well. Therefore do not worry about tomorrow, for tomorrow will worry about itself. Each day has enough trouble of its own.

When we look to God's Word, we can see that He tells us very clearly what we are to seek after, and it leads us to the first must-pack of The Freshman 15. It is to:

1ST MUST-PACK: SEEK GOD FIRST

What does it mean to seek God first, really? What is this verse saying to us and how do we apply it? Let's take a closer look.

In this passage, the people are troubled about three main things, what are they? What they will:

1. _____

2. _____

3. _____

The people were concerned about what they were going to eat, drink and wear. These three things may not be on the top of your worry list, but you could easily replace the three worries of the people from this passage with the three concerns you listed in the introduction.

The scripture goes on to say that the way these people dealt with their concerns was by worrying over them or, in our terms, letting it "stress them out." And to make matters worse, then they ran after the very things causing their worry! It said, "For the pagans RUN after all these things…"

Strong's Greek and Hebrew dictionary defines "run" in this context as epizeteo:

1) to enquire for, seek for, search for, seek diligently

2) to wish for, crave

3) to demand, clamor for

These pagans were craving, wishing for and clamoring after the things they needed instead of seeking the Creator and Provider of all they could ever need.

Instead of worrying about our daily needs, the scripture tells us that our concern should be about the things of God. Specifically, His kingdom and His righteousness are to be our chief concerns. Remember this scripture as you face your freshman year because it will be very easy to "seek after" other things.

What are other things you could see yourself seeking or running after in college instead of the Lord and His Kingdom? (Circle any that apply)

Guys/Dating	Grades	Friends	Popularity
Physical perfection	Jobs	Money	Fun
Accomplishments	Pleasing others	Other:_____	

We could also call the things we "seek after" our main concerns. When we place anything besides the Lord as our main concern, we will find ourselves frustrated and empty. However, when we seek to know and serve the Lord, we find that He takes care of our every concern.

The Message paraphrases the final verses of our Matthew 6 passage like this:

> What I'm trying to do here is to get you to relax, to not be so preoccupied with *getting*, so you can respond to God's *giving*. People who don't know God and the way he works fuss over these things, but you know both God and how he works. Steep your life in <u>God-reality, God-initiative, God-provisions.</u> Don't worry about missing out. You'll find all your everyday human concerns will be met.

> Give your entire attention to what God is doing right now, and don't get worked up about what may or may not happen tomorrow. God will help you deal with whatever hard things come up when the time comes (emphasis mine).

Please read the paraphrase one more time. I don't want you to miss the power of this passage. I have already taken this translation and taped it to my bathroom mirror so that I look at it every morning. I need the daily reminder that *I do know God and how He works!* Because of that, I KNOW He will meet all of my everyday needs. I don't need to get worked up over the getting, but rather focus on Him and what HE is giving! What part of this passage do you feel you need to remember today?

Let's break this scripture down further and take a look at the word **steep** in verse 33.

When I think of *steep*, I think about making tea. Being from the Texas, I love strong, sweet tea. To make good 'ole Southern, sweet tea, all you need is a pitcher, a lot of sugar, a pot or kettle of boiling water, and a couple of big tea bags. Once the water has finished boiling, you take the tea bags, dunk them in the hot water and let them STEEP. Steeping the tea means that you let those tea bags completely immerse themselves in the hot water and let the water soak the tea bag. Dear friend, I know that this may sound strange, but we must be like those tea bags! God is calling us to jump into the Living Water and completely immerse ourselves so that we are saturated with all that He is.

For an accurate definition of the word "steep", I went to dictionary.com and found this definition in relation to the context of our passage:

> steep[2] – *verb (used with object)* to immerse in or saturate or imbue with some pervading, absorbing, or stupefying influence or agency

When we continue reading the passage, we are told that we must immerse or steep our lives in three things. Refer back to the passage to complete the blanks:

"Steep your lives in…"

1. God-_____

2. God-_____

3. God-_____

Our scripture doesn't say anything about saturating ourselves with shoe shopping, husband finding, awesome grade getting or anything but **God-Reality, God-Initiative,** and **God-Provisions**. Essentially, this passage is showing us to replace the three earthly concerns of the people that we listed earlier with an eternal focus.

There is a great example in scripture of two women who were seeking. One sought after and tried to absorb all she could of the right thing, the Lord Jesus, and the other was caught up in busily seeking after earthly things.

These two women were Mary and Martha. Let's take a look at their story in Luke 10:38-41:

> While they were traveling, He entered a village, and a woman named Martha welcomed Him into her home. She had a sister named Mary, who also sat at the Lord's feet and was listening to what He said. But Martha was distracted by her many tasks, and she came up and asked, "Lord, don't You care that my sister has left me to serve alone? So tell her to give me a hand."
>
> The Lord answered her, "Martha, Martha, you are worried and upset about many things, but one thing is necessary. Mary has made the right choice, and it will not be taken away from her." (HCSB)

What was Martha's chief concern? _____

What was Mary's chief concern? _____

Who did Jesus say had chosen correctly? _____

Here's what *Baker Exegetical Commentary on the New Testament* had to say about this passage:

> Jesus' visit with Mary and Martha is an object lesson on the priority of responding to Jesus over worldly concerns. Luke 10:38-42 highlights a major feature of discipleship: choosing to order one's affairs properly. One of the facts of life is that its demands are often all consuming. In fact, much of life is spent fulfilling these demands. Such was Martha's situation when Jesus visited her. She was diligent in preparing an appropriate meal for the teacher. In contrast, Mary simply sat down. She was not lifting a finger to help, and Martha was disturbed. But Mary had made the right choice, according to Jesus. **The disciple who reflects on Jesus' teaching receives a meal that is never removed.** To sit at Jesus' feet is the disciple's priority. The worries of life should never prevent one from consuming God's word. This is Luke's message to disciples: sit at Jesus' feet and devour his teaching, since there is no more important meal" (p. 1037, 1042-1043, emphasis mine).

Wow! Did you catch that it said that partaking in the words of Christ, The Bread of Life, is our most important meal? Do you remember that worrying about what they were going to eat was one of the major worries listed in our Matthew 6 passage? Dear ladies, let us imitate Mary. When we begin to feel the desire to worry over earthly things, may we stop and sit at the feet of Jesus and learn from Him. That is how we seek Him first and trust that everything else will be added.

Doing that brings us to the 2nd must-pack in this session:

2ND MUST-PACK:
SPEND TIME WITH THE LORD

This means that we talk to God and read and study His Word. I want to warn you that this is so essential and unfortunately, so easy to neglect. You've probably heard this personal time with God referred to as your "Quiet Time" or "Daily Devotional".

Growing up in the church, I heard the phrase "spend time with the Lord" so much but I don't think I fully understood why it was so important. In case you are in the same boat, let's look at a few of the many reasons why this is so vital, especially in your college years. The main reason is that prayer and reading God's Word are the two main ways in which we communicate with God. Let me explain it like this:

Think of your best friend: What are three things you and your best friend do together that make you so close?

1.

2.

3.

You might have answered that you spend time together, talk on the phone, text each other, write each other notes and post comments on each other's Facebook. What if you didn't do those things? What if your friend sent you a text message every day for a week and you didn't read them? What if your friend asked you to hang out and you didn't go? What if she called you and you didn't answer? Would you be very close? NO. If you weren't doing the things that helped you communicate and bond, you wouldn't know what was going on with your friend. Our relationship with Jesus is similar. We must read the notes He sent us, which can be found in the Bible. We must also talk to Him through prayer.

The Bible gives us several more reasons why it is important to spend time with Him. Please draw a line connecting the reason with the scripture.

Jesus, our example, did so	Hebrews 4:14-16
We find all we need for life and godliness	Jeremiah 15:16
Provides guidance and direction	Luke 5:16
Offers help in time of need	Psalm 119:105
So that you can detect a fake	2 Peter 1:3-4
The joy found in studying scripture	2 Timothy 4:3-4

Please know that this is just a short list of the many reasons why we benefit from knowing God's Word. When we spend time with Him, we find that our questions about His will for our lives are answered, the things that are worrying us are replaced with His peace, our burdens and struggles are lifted and our lives are filled with joy as we fall more in love with Him. I want to touch on another major reason why it is important for you to study the scriptures.

College is a place of research, study and a gathering of many great thinkers from many different backgrounds and belief systems. It is basically created to be in many ways a testing ground of who you are and what you believe. Your friends, classmates and professors will challenge your beliefs, and it is essential that YOU KNOW WHAT YOU BELIEVE.

This reminds me of something I heard once about the FBI and how they check for counterfeit money. Did you know that FBI agents don't spend any time studying fake money? Instead, they study the real thing. They take genuine, authentic American money and then memorize all its parts. They feel it, let it run through their fingers. They simply focus all of their efforts on studying the real thing, so that when a counterfeit presents itself, they will immediately know it is a fake.

You and I must be so familiar with scripture that when someone attacks our beliefs or tries to convince us of something untrue, we can immediately detect it as a fake! I'm not saying that you shouldn't study other religions because it is helpful in relating to people of other beliefs. However, I am challenging you to study scripture in such a way that when someone tries to pass off something that may look very similar but is not the real thing, you will know it immediately.

Hopefully, I've made it pretty clear that this time with the Lord is very important! It's so important that you may find that you have to fight for your alone time with God like never before. In order to help you be prepared for how you are going to ensure that you have this time, I want you to answer a few questions:

1.   When are you going to have your devotionals? (Circle One)

        Morning   Noon   Night

2.   Where are you going to have your devotionals? (Be specific)

3.   What are you going to study?

4.   Are you going to keep a journal?

I really encourage you to make sure that this must-pack makes it in your suitcase and that you use it daily. It is too easy to get busy and forget it. There may be times when you a miss a day or two or even a week or two, but please do not let that discourage you and cause you to give up on it all together. Just start again the next day. The Lord is waiting and ready to spend time with you.

So far, we've solidified the truths that we must **Seek God First** and the way we do that is by **Spending Time with the Lord**. However, it doesn't end there. God did not intend for you to live the Christian life alone. He has called you to participate in "the body". Seeking after God on your own in a world where it's not always the cool thing to do is hard. That is why He calls us to partner up with other believers, a group of people called the Church. Our third must-pack in our list of 15 is:

3RD 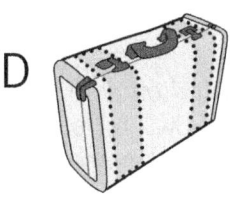 MUST-PACK:
GET PLUGGED INTO A LOCAL CHURCH

Not only is it essential that you have a personal, growing relationship with the Lord, it is vital that you are involved with a community of believers that will help guide you, encourage you, teach you and provide a place for you to serve.

The summer before I left for college, I sought the counsel of a very wise, Christian woman. One of the things she told me that really stood out was that I needed to build bridges from my current home to my new college home. She emphasized the importance of building a bridge between my current church home and what would be my new church home while I was in college. I took her words to heart and began the search for a church.

I was going to attend my freshman year at a little college in Erie, Pennsylvania, called Mercyhurst. Erie was my father's hometown and where my grandparents still lived, which meant we had visited there often. At home, I found an Erie phonebook (yes, that is when we still used those ancient things we called phonebooks) and went to the section of the yellow pages titled "Churches."

I had been praying for God to lead me to a church in Erie and continued to pray as my eyes scanned across the pages listing all of the churches from every denomination, hoping that somehow one would stand out to me. Some of the churches had descriptions, mission statements, church service times and I took care to read whatever each church posted about itself. Then, my eyes fell on a particular outlined advertisement for Grace Bible Church and I felt a stirring in my spirit. I went to the computer to look up the website they had listed in the ad. I remember looking at the website, reading information about the churches beliefs, mission statement, ministries, staff members and then soaking it all in and praying for direction from the Lord to know if this is where He would want me to serve.

After praying about it, I decided to give Derek Sanford, the youth pastor listed on the website, a call and see if they might need any help in their youth group the following year. Derek was so kind to me and was excited about my arrival. I gave him the date of the weekend my parents would be moving me to Erie and told him that we would be at church that Sunday. It brought me such peace to know that I had a fellowship waiting for me.

After the service, Derek picked me out of the crowd and introduced himself to my family and me. He gave me a tour of the church and introduced me to many of the youth staff members. I knew from that moment on that the Lord had provided a place for me to call "home" as I was so many thousand miles from what I had known as home. As if they had known me my whole life, they welcomed me into the fold. My new friends took care of me and provided a place of refuge and encouragement. They took me to movies, to dinner, to youth stuff, running at the lake and to an unforgettable N'Sync concert! That group of people impacted my freshman year more than anyone I would encounter on campus.

Involvement in a church in your local area is easily neglected. Too many college freshmen think they will just go to the church in their hometown when they visit on weekends and that will be enough. Don't be deceived, you must find a church home in the new town where you are living. The church is very important to God, and you as a part of it, serve a unique purpose.

As I was studying to teach a Sunday school lesson a few weeks ago, I came across this explanation of the church and wanted to share it with you. It said:

> Ultimately, the church is God's plan for taking the gospel to the entire world. By building up its members in Christlikeness through the instruction of God's Word, fellowship, service, worship, and prayer, the Church is an unstoppable force when it comes to glorifying God. (Student Life Bible Study from the study of Community from Lesson 1: What is the Church?)

Another helpful explanation of our role in the body comes from *How to Stay Christian in College*:

> When the Bible says the church is the body of Christ, it's telling you that during the present age, those who are united with Christ are the physical means by which *He* acts in the world. They are His way of doing things, *His* way of making *His* will come to pass. The hands, the feet, the legs, and all the other parts – all of them depend on each other and all of them have tasks for the good of the whole. You do, too (p. 145).

In case you missed it before, please remember: It is crucial that you locate and get involved in a church body *where you are going to college*. The problem that occurs with so many of us as we are looking for a new church home is that we approach the search the same way we approach the make-up counter in the mall.

The scenario goes a little like this: you walk up to the counter and take a seat in a stylish but comfy black leather chair trimmed in stainless steel and wait for someone to wait on you as you survey the buffet of options set before you. The cosmetics lady sees you waiting and comes over to you and asks, "What is it you are looking for today?" You may tell her a little about the colors that you have been using and why you liked some of them and have begun to dislike others. You then ask her what new shades she has to offer you in the blush you have grown tired of but tell her that you are going to stick with Flirty Flutter for your lip gloss. Together, the two of you work through the assortment of colors, hues and flavors that you need in your make-up bag until you have selected your new, perfect, custom look.

Too often, we see the church search like this make-up counter. We pick and choose from what we like and don't like, ultimately looking for what is "best for me." We are ready to get rid of the things we didn't like in our old church and to find a new church with all of the bells and whistles we have been wanting. We are willing to shop around until we find that new, perfect, custom church. Ladies, for the make-up counter this is fine, but in finding a church, this is an unacceptable attitude. As you search for your new church home, do not let this be your method.

Because we live in a society in which we can pretty much hand pick everything we want, we translate that mentality to the church. We go into a church that we're "trying out" and take with us a little scorecard. We rate the worship: *Is it my type of music? Do they have instruments? Do they sing hymns or modern choruses?* Then, we rate the preacher: *Is he funny? Is he young or old? Is he entertaining?* We rate the people at the service. We rate the building. We rate the programs offered.

We walk out of service with the score we gave them and prepare to try another church the next weekend and repeat the same technique all over again. Ladies, I have to tell you that this the wrong approach for finding a church. When we use it, we feel very unsettled and allow the Enemy an opportunity to keep us from getting plugged in because we are never able to give a church a perfect "10." We never get involved, we never fellowship with a body of believers and therefore, we fail to grow as we could.

So if we are not supposed to have a custom-made church mentality, what kind of attitude should we have and what should we look for?
Here are a few good questions to ask about the churches you are thinking of joining:

1. Does it match up with your beliefs?
   You can typically go to the church's website to find their belief statement. If you come across anything you're concerned about, give your youth pastor or pastor from your last church a call and see what they think.

2. Is this a place where you are going to be fed and be able to grow in your faith?

3. Is this a place where you have an opportunity to serve?

4. Do you have peace from the Holy Spirit about joining this body of believers?

This is not an exhaustive list, but it should get you started in your search. Now that you know the right mindset in finding a new church home, I want to ask you a few questions about how you're going to find it.

- Do you know of any churches where your college is located?

     YES or NO

- Have you found any churches you want to visit?

     Name of Church:

- When are you going to visit those churches?

- What ministries are you interested in being involved with and/or serving in?
  (Circle One)

Media/Technology	Youth	Praise Team
College Women's Prayer Team	Children	Other: _____

If some of these questions are hard for you to answer right now, then it's time for you to get busy! Start researching the churches available in your college town. If you're still having trouble by the time school starts, be on the lookout for organizations on your campus that set up tables at orientation to tell you about ministries available to you. I know of several colleges that do this to help students find a college ministry at local churches. This can be very helpful in finding a group of Christian friends and a place to call your new church home.

One thing I want to warn you about is not replacing church with your on-campus ministry or Bible Study. Campuses usually offer many ways to get involved and minister to your school. I recommend finding ONE where you could serve but make sure that you are attending your church and serving there. Like we discussed earlier, God has called you to participate in His Body, the church, and it is important that you do not neglect that calling.

Here we are, ladies, at the end of this chapter, Keeping the Faith. We have laid a firm foundation.

Do you remember the first three must-packs of The Freshman 15? If so, write them in here:

1ST MUST-PACK:_____

2ND MUST-PACK:_____

3RD MUST-PACK:_____

These are the founding principles. We can't build from here unless it is very clear to you that God must be first and foremost in our hearts and lives. We have to seek Him and know Him more by spending time in His Word, the Bible. We also must link up with other believers and find a place to serve in the body. Ladies, college will be a whole new world. Please allow the Lord to be your Guide through it all. He is the only way you will find lasting peace, security and direction in your college years and throughout your life.

We have lots more we need to make sure gets in our college-bound suitcase! If you're worried you don't have the time to do it all, just turn to the next chapter. We'll discuss time management, and I'll teach you a few tools to make sure you have the time to do the three things we've talked about.

TIME MANAGE —MENT

College is the "Land of Opportunity!" Truly, you may never have more opportunities available to you than you will during your college years. You will be presented with options to join sororities, churches, Bible studies, academic clubs, sports teams and an array of other groups. Doors will be opened for you to take classes that you really enjoy and some that you may not enjoy but know that you need. You'll find opportunities to get jobs and internships. You'll have a slew of new friends who offer all kinds of things to keep you busy. They'll invite you to dorm gatherings, football games, socials, "study" groups (although there may not be much studying done!), parties—the list goes on.

With all of these opportunities at your disposal, you must take advantage of them. However, you have to be intentional about where you choose to focus your time. The pitfall that many college students encounter is that they are so involved and so busy that they struggle to find success in any of the areas they spend their time. If they would take a moment to look around, they would realize that they are not really getting anywhere or accomplishing much of anything.

This makes me think of my favorite class offered at my gym; spin class. "Spin" is an hour-long class of intense riding on a stationary bike with a room full of other lunatics on stationary bikes. Everyone starts the class excited and ready to ride but I have to tell you that by the time we leave, everyone is drenched in sweat, panting for more water because we have already finished off the bottle we brought and ready to go home and get in the shower. To help distract us from the pain, the instructor cranks up the fast beat, thumping tunes and yells at us periodically to turn up the intensity. To keep myself from surrendering to my exhaustion during this wild-ride, I have to picture myself out riding through the mountains or along a beach. I have to close my eyes and pretend that I am actually going somewhere. Because although I should be halfway to Canada by the end of class, I'm still in the same spot I started! I think that if I were to really grasp the fact that I was pedaling with all my might, yet going NOWHERE, I might go insane!

This insanity is so much like what we do, especially in the Christian life and to an even greater degree in our college years. We are presented with all of these great opportunities and we say "yes" to everything. Eventually, like the frantic pedaling on the bike, we get so busy trying to satisfy each of our obligations that we are not actually getting anything productive done with any *one* of them.

I remember a time in college where I went Bible study crazy. During the same semester, I joined the Bible study in my Christian sorority, a Bible study with a group of friends, a Bible study with my college group at church and was teaching Sunday school and studying for that. Do you think I grew significantly in my walk during that time? No way! I was so busy completing Bible studies that really all I was doing was finishing them. I wasn't able to concentrate on any *one* of them and allow the truths of the study to make a change in my life. It was as if I was sitting on that stationary bike, pedaling as fast as I could and getting nowhere.

Scripture talks about this very thing. Let's take a look in 1 Corinthians 9:24-27 where it says:

> Do you not know that in a race all the runners run, but only one gets the prize? Run in such a way as to get the prize.

> Everyone who competes in the games goes into strict training. They do it to get a crown that will not last; but we do it to get a crown that will last forever. *Therefore I do not run like a man running aimlessly; I do not fight like a man beating the air.* No, I beat my body and make it my slave so that after I have preached to others, I myself will not be disqualified for the prize (emphasis mine).

The author of this passage is Paul, a man who knew his calling and sought to fulfill it with great determination. What was Paul's calling? Acts 9:15 says that the Lord called Paul "to carry my name before the Gentiles and their kings and before the people of Israel." Paul knew his calling and focused his efforts accordingly. Paul compares the way that he lived for Christ like a runner in a race.

How did Paul run the race? (Circle one)

Without purpose   Wherever he felt like running   With focus and purpose

He knew that God had called him to preach the gospel and therefore, he made decisions to live out that calling with focus and purpose.

As we make decisions about how we are going to spend our time, we must know our purpose. Paul's purpose was very clear to him. He had received a special message from the Lord telling him exactly what he needed to do. Do you realize that your purpose is actually very similar to Paul's and was sent as a special message to you? We might summarize our calling like this: to glorify God by getting to know Him and making Him known. How do I know that Paul's calling is the same as that for all Christians? I know it because I find it in scripture. If we read what is known as **The Greatest Commandment**, we find that it says:

> … love the Lord your God with all your **heart** and with all your **soul** and with all your **mind** and with all your **strength**.' The second is this: 'Love your neighbor as yourself.' There is no commandment greater than these (Mark 12:30-31, emphasis mine).

Another "great" in scripture where we find our purpose is **The Great Commission**:

> Therefore go and make **disciples** of all nations, **baptizing** them in the name of the Father and of the Son and of the Holy Spirit, and **teaching** them to obey everything I have commanded you. And surely I am with you always, to the very end of the age (Matthew 28:19-20, emphasis mine).

What are the two "greats" in scripture that help us to know our purpose?

The Greatest _____ :

Love the Lord your God with all your _____, _____, _____ and _____

The Great _____ :

1. Go and make _____ of all nations

2. _____ them in the name of the Father and of the Son and of the Holy Spirit

3. _____ them to obey everything I have commanded you

Paul knew that God had called him to preach the gospel and therefore, he made decisions to live out that calling. You, dear one, have that same calling. Your job is to make sure that you are fulfilling that calling wherever you are. For now, it means that you do that in and through your time in college. You must choose from all of the opportunities available. How best can you use the gifts God has given you to live out your purpose?

This brings us to the 4th must-pack of The Freshman 15, which is to:

4TH MUST-PACK:
BE EFFECTIVE BY BEING SELECTIVE

I remember coming across this phrase when I was reading *The Purpose Driven Life* by Rick Warren. Warren goes on to explain the power in this must-pack by saying:

> The power of focusing can be seen in light. Diffused light has little power or impact, but you can concentrate its energy by focusing it. With a magnifying glass, the rays of the sun can be focused to set grass or paper on fire. When light is focused even more as a laser beam, it can cut through steel.
>
> There is nothing quite as potent as a focused life, one lived on purpose. The men and women who have made the greatest difference in history were the most focused. For instance, the apostle Paul almost single-handedly spread Christianity throughout the Roman Empire. His secret was a focused life. He said, 'I am focusing all my energies on this one thing: Forgetting the past and looking forward to what lies ahead.'
>
> If you want your life to have impact, focus it! Stop dabbling. Stop trying to do it all. Do less. Prune away even the good activities and do only that which matters most. Never confuse activity with productivity. You can be busy without a purpose, but what's the point? Paul said, 'Let's keep focused on the goal, those of us who want everything God has for us' (p. 32).

Let's get a little historical. Think back on your high school years. Can you think of a time when you were either too involved or just too busy? What activities were you doing? How did it make you feel?

Please explain what that was like:

A life spinning out of control is no fun at all. It is exhausting and unfulfilling. I want to help you avoid that daily insanity by helping you focus. I want you to live on purpose, fulfilling The Greatest Commandment and The Great Commission. The way we live out that purpose is by using the gifts God has given each of us.

Did you know that you have been given spiritual gifts from the Holy Spirit? The Bible has lots to say about the various spiritual gifts we have been given. Check out Romans 12:6-8; 1 Corinthians 12:8-10, 28-30; Ephesians 4:11; and 1 Peter 4:9-11. 1 Peter 4:10 tells us that we are to use the gifts we have received to serve others. Gene Wilkes defines the purpose of spiritual gifts as "an expression of the Holy Spirit in the life of believers which empowers them to serve the body of Christ, the church." Awareness of our spiritual giftedness is key when we are deciding where and how to spend our time. There has been a great deal written about spiritual gifts and if you have further interest, I challenge you to continue your study of this topic.

You may know which gifts you have by thinking about ways in which you feel the most satisfied and effective in serving. Listed below is a concise list of the spiritual gifts found in scripture. Please read over them. Then, take a moment to pray and ask the Holy Spirit to help you understand which of these you have been specifically gifted with. Place a check mark next to any of the gifts that you believe apply to you.

_____**Leadership** (Rom. 12:8)	_____**Hospitality** (1 Pet. 4:9)
_____**Administration** (1 Cor. 12:28)	_____**Giving** (Rom. 12:8)
_____**Encouragement** (Rom. 12:8)	_____**Faith** (1 Cor. 12:9)
_____**Shepherding** (Eph. 4:11)	_____**Mercy** (Rom. 12:8)
_____**Preaching** (1Cor. 12:10; Rom. 12:6)	_____**Wisdom** (1 Cor. 12:28)
_____**Evangelism** (Eph. 4:11)	_____**Service/Helps** (1 Cor. 12:28; Rom. 12:7)
_____**Teaching** (1 Cor. 12:28; Eph. 4:11)	_____**Foreign Missions** (1 Cor.12:28; Eph. 4:11)

(List taken from: Gene Wilkes, Discover Your Spiritual Gifts. http://www.lifeway.com/lwc/files/lwcF_wmn_SpiritualGifts_List.pdf)

Did a few gifts stand out to you? Make sure you put checks next to the ones you have, not necessarily the ones you want! For instance, I believe I have been gifted with teaching but I lack the gift of administration and would love if it came more naturally to me. However, knowing that about myself, I don't take on roles as an administrator. I know that if I am really needed, the Holy Spirit will intervene but if there is one more gifted than me available, I let that person have the job. I have found that I am truly more effective when I am selective with the things I say "yes" to and my giftedness plays a major role in the selection process.

Before we move on, I want to give you a resource in case you need more help discovering your spiritual giftedness. I found this Spiritual Gifts Survey through lifeway.com. You can either search lifeway.com for Spiritual Gifts Survey or type in this link:

http://www.lifeway.com/lwc/files/lwcF_wmn_SpiritualGifts_Survey.pdf

Let's take a look back. I want to make sure this is so clear in your mind before we take on the next must-pack in our 15. Please fill in the blanks below based on what you've just read:

We become more effective by being _____.

We use our spiritual _____ to help us in the selection process.

Did you remember? I hope so because in this new "Land of Opportunity," we have to keep our eyes focused on our purpose and not get distracted by the Enemy. If you're ready, let's pack our next item. With all of these new opportunities available to you, you must pack the fifth item of The Freshman 15:

5TH MUST-PACK:
REST

Rest is a pretty simple instruction that is lost on too many of us. This must-pack is going to involve sleep, which we will talk about a little later, but *resting* is found in scripture and is essential to our success. Scripture teaches about two types of rest that are necessary. One is a mindset, a constant way of living, and the other is the act of being refreshed.
Scripture refers to both types of rest several times.

First, let's examine the type of rest called the Sabbath Mindset. Remember that God commanded the Israelites to take a Sabbath (cease from work) on the seventh day of each week to follow God's example after His work of creating the world in six days and then resting. For the Israelites, any work they did on the Sabbath was considered sin. We know that when Christ came to Earth, he fulfilled all of the laws that the Israelites were living under. One of these laws He fulfilled was the law concerning the Sabbath. What does that mean for us? It means that we don't have to wait until Sunday to rest! It means that we can find this Sabbath-rest constantly as we live in Christ. How amazing! We have the opportunity, through the indwelling of the Holy Spirit, to live in a continual state of rest, or peace, with the Lord. Matthew 11:28-30 is a scripture where we see Jesus teach about this type of rest:

> Come to Me, all you who are weary and burdened, and I will give you rest. Take My yoke upon you and learn from Me, because I am gentle and humble in heart, and you will find rest for your souls. For My yoke is easy and My burden is light.

J. Patrick Hastings' Bible Dictionary explains:

> Christ's 'rest' is not a 'rest' from work, but in work, "not the rest of inactivity but of the harmonious working of all the faculties and affections, of will, heart, imagination, conscience, because each has found in God the ideal sphere for its satisfaction and development.

You see, we find rest in Christ as we serve Him, *while* we work. We must rely on Him to give us that rest in our work to keep us free from stress and anxiety. If you recall, we talked about this same concept in our first must-pack: Seek God First. This is the same idea but is important enough to be discussed again. You may find that your freshman year is the busiest time of your life, but the great gift we have in Christ is that though we may be outwardly active, we are inwardly still. This rest is one that we have to come to Christ and take from Him. It must be sought after.

One day, when we finally reach our Heavenly destination, we will enter the true and complete rest for our souls (Hebrews 4:1-11). We will find a place in which we experience no more trouble and no more worry. Hallelujah! For now, on this Earth, God allows us to experience a taste of that Heavenly rest through our relationship with Christ.

The second type of rest occurs when we cease working and seek refreshment. The problem with this type of rest is that it is often misunderstood and may even be perceived as laziness. Our culture sees activity as productivity, meaning the busier you are the more successful you must surely be. This is not so! Please do not fall into this trap.

Just as we talked about earlier with the example from my spinning class, you can be spinning your wheels as fast as you can and not be productive. You must learn to be still and find time to be refreshed. This idea is not celebrated in our culture and is especially unpopular on college campuses.

It appears that on most college campuses, you will find one of either two extremes. You either have the super-busy, hyped up on Red Bull girl that is running around from class to class and social event to social event in a maddening display of over-worked, under-rested mania. Or we find the couch potato. The slug that lies in bed all day, sleeps in, skips class, updates their Facebook status every five minutes with "is doing nothing" and yet always seems tired. What I am challenging you to do is to strike a balance—to live in such a way that you are *productive with a purpose and restful for refreshment.*

There are consequences when you don't find time to rest. Remember our Red Bull girl from before? Sure, she's flying high now, but what happens after a week or a month of such hyperactivity? I've seen it happen too many times and often through a mirror reflection. Things seem to be going along just fine until…the crash. Inevitably, all of this mania will lead to a sudden halt when something happens that throws you off of the bike on which you've been pedaling so fast. You stop and wonder why you were doing all of this at such an intense rate in the first place. For me, the question I would have to ask myself is, "For *who* am I doing all of this?" I would quickly realize that I was trying to appear like Productive Patty to all of those around me when really I was feeling much more like Insecure Irene.

Where are you on the scale of productivity? Circle the place on the line that most accurately describes you:

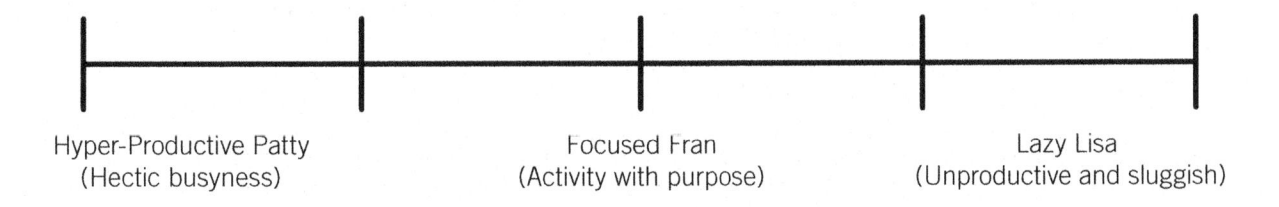

Hyper-Productive Patty   Focused Fran   Lazy Lisa
(Hectic busyness)   (Activity with purpose)   (Unproductive and sluggish)

In the middle of my madness, I would have to stop and sit down with the Lord and get right about my motives. And then, like always, when I turned over the reigns of my life to Him, I would be able to find rest and peace for my soul.

Let's talk about how living a restful life looks like for you. We already talked about living with a Sabbath Mindset, and I mentioned that the other way we find rest in our lives is by doing things that refresh us. Although sleep is necessary and we are about to talk about it, we are going to focus here on activities that refresh. Remember my spin class? After pedaling hard for a while, I would realize that I needed a drink. A dry, panting mouth would remind me that I needed a little refreshment. I would put my hand around that cold, plastic bottle, unscrew the top and allow that revitalizing liquid to run down my throat and quench my thirst. That's what we're talking about here. You've been pedaling hard and it's time to get a drink, to get refreshed. What would that look like for you? I've listed below some activities that may be refreshing to you. Please circle any that apply and add any others.

Going for a walk	Journaling	Reading	Singing
Spending time in the Word	Taking a bath	Talking with an encouraging believer	
Playing an instrument	Crafting/Creative activity		Praying

Others: _____

Did you notice that I didn't list TV, Facebook, the internet, video games, or computer stuff on here? That's because I have found that those activities are not truly refreshing to me. When I'm feeling tired, my first inclination may be to turn on the TV. However, when I turn it off and get back to work, I don't feel any better or more rested than I did before. Don't misunderstand me. I enjoy my time on the internet, playing Wii and watching TV. I put those things under the "leisure activities" category. Be careful not to confuse the two. One is fun and helps pass the time but the other helps to fuel you so that you have the energy for the work and the fun.

We've talked about two types of rest so far: living in the Sabbath mindset and participating in refreshing activity. Now, as promised, we are going to talk about sleep. Sleep, for whatever reason, has become "uncool" on college campuses. Students seem to think that the less sleep you get the more fun you must be having or the better student you must be. Don't believe the lie! The truth is that sleep is so important to your success and effectiveness and that makes it very COOL! (Please excuse my cheesiness, I just couldn't resist!)

A Brown University article gave the statistic for the percentage of college students with good sleep quality. What would you guess the percentage is?

2%   11%   25%   52%

The answer: 11%! Only a small portion of college students are getting an adequate amount of sleep. The article revealed that eight hours is the average need for a college student but that most students are only getting about six hours of sleep.

What's the big deal? Why is sleep so important? The article listed some of the side effects to sleep deprivation:

1. Weakens immune system (you'll get sick easier)
2. Affects mental health which may cause tension, irritability and depression
3. Diminishes classroom performance
4. Impairs driving ability (driving while tired is as dangerous as driving while intoxicated!)

Article found at: http://www.brown.edu/Student_Services/Health_Services/Health_Education/general_health/sleep.htm

What's my point? SLEEP! You have to sleep and you need to try and get eight hours. Your body will love you and give you the strength and energy you need if you try and turn in at the same time every night and get up at the same time every morning. If you're thinking, "I'm not going to have time to sleep! I'm going to be so busy trying to get all of the things done on my new college sized to-do list," then stay tuned!

In order to ensure that you get the rest you need and that you have time to be effective in the activities you have selected, we are going to add our next must-pack to our college suitcase.

6TH MUST-PACK:
SCHEDULE YOUR TIME

When we start to think about scheduling our time, we have to first establish our priorities. Below, I've listed some things that might make your list of top 5. Please look over the list, add any that are priorities for you that are not listed and then write them in the space provided. Don't worry about putting them in order of importance or trying to answer based on what you think you *should* write.

| Family | Church | Exercising | School | God | Internet |
| Fun | Job | Friends | Ministry | Other:_____ |

Top Five Priorities

1.

2.

3.

4.

5.

Now, I want you to think about a typical day and add up how many minutes or hours in a day that you concentrate on each of the five priorities you listed. Write the amount of time in parenthesis after the item.

Your list may look a little like this:
1. Family (2 hours)
2. God (30 minutes)
3. School (7 hours)
4. Friends (1 hr 30 minutes)
5. Church (1 hour)

Look at the time spent on your list. Does your time spent on each item reflect that they are a priority? Keep in mind that you are a student and as much as you would like to, you may not be able to spend three hours with your family or have two-hour long devotionals! I just want you to keep these things that are important to you in mind as we make our schedule. We have to be intentional about where we spend our time because when we don't, we tend to piddle our time away on things that don't matter. We can call these TIME WASTERS.

Time waster activities aren't necessarily bad things to spend time doing. However, what often happens with these activities is that we sit down to spend a few minutes doing them and several hours later realize that we never got to our homework and now have to go to bed!

So, think about it. What might be a time waster for you? Circle the items below that waste your time:

Internet	Facebook	Texting	Watching TV
Pinterest	Chatting	Talking on the phone	

Playing games on the computer   Other: _____

Now, next to the items you circled, write in parenthesis approximately how much time you spend doing them each day.

Do you see what I'm trying to get you to realize? I want you to have a clearer picture of how you spend your time. If we don't stop periodically and look at where the hours of are day are going, we start just living life and surviving each day instead of being intentional about where we spend our time and *thriving each day!* If you said that you spent a lot of time on the internet and especially on social networking sites like Pinterest or Facebook, you are not alone! A quick search about time wasters on the internet will prove that people of all ages and walks of life are doing the same thing. Some sites even show that the average college student spends anywhere from two to eight hours on social networking sites.

Let me clarify one more time. I'm not saying that anything in the above list is a BAD thing. When you plan them in and they count as your leisure activities, they are perfectly appropriate. But let's be real, ladies. It's when we have a paper we are supposed to write or a test we are supposed to study for that these little time wasters creep in and cause us to squander away a lot of time.

We use our time wasters to procrastinate. What does this word procrastinate mean? I think it was on a vocab test I was supposed to study for but I kept putting it off until I didn't have any time to actually study the word. Well, then, you procrastinated! Procrastination is when we put something off until another time. For me, procrastination is a slippery slope and it probably is for you, too. When I procrastinate on an assignment, I may begin to feel anxious, depressed and worried and it affects my success on the assignment. I may say to myself, "I'm just gonna watch one more show and then I'll get started" or "I really need to respond to all of these messages in my inbox. I've really been putting that off. Then, I'll start on my paper." I can tell you that the longer I try to avoid the assignment, the more anxious I feel. Besides that, do you think I enjoyed that one last TV show? No! The upcoming paper I had to write was looming over me! Has this ever happened to you? Have you ever said or felt any of the things I mentioned? If so, you've just been diagnosed with procrastinitus. But don't fret, I have the cure! It's called TIME MANAGEMENT!

What we have to do, to avoid these bad feelings surrounding procrastination, is to make a schedule. To begin our schedule, we have to figure out what our "big rocks" and our "little rocks" are. I got this idea from a time management expert, Stephen Covey. Here's how he explains it in his book *First Things First:*

In the middle of a seminar on time management, the lecturer said, "Okay, it's time for a quiz." Reaching under the table, he pulled out a wide mouthed gallon jar and set it on the table next to a platter covered with fist-sized rocks. "How many of these rocks do you think we can get in the jar?" he asked the audience.

After the students made their guesses, the seminar leader said, "Okay, let's find out." He put one rock in the jar, then another, then another--until no more rocks would fit. Then he asked, "Is the jar full?"

Everybody could see that not one more of the rocks would fit, so they said, "Yes."

"Not so fast," he cautioned. From under the table he lifted out a bucket of gravel, dumped it in the jar, and shook it. The gravel slid into all the little spaces left by the big rocks. Grinning, the seminar leader asked once more, "Is the jar full?"

A little wiser by now, the students responded, "Probably not." "Good," the teacher said. Then he reached under the table to bring up a bucket of sand. He started dumping the sand in the jar. While the students watched, the sand filled in the little spaces left by the rocks and gravel. Once more he looked at the class and said, "Now, is the jar full?"

"No," everyone shouted back.

"Good!" said the seminar leader, who then grabbed a pitcher of water and began to pour it into the jar. He got something like a quart of water into that jar before he said, "Ladies and gentlemen, the jar is now full. Can anybody tell me the lesson you can learn from this?

What's my point?"

An eager participant spoke up: "Well, there are gaps in your schedule. And if you really work at it, you can always fit more into your life."

"No," the leader said. "That's not the point. The point is this: if I hadn't put those big rocks in first, I would never have gotten them in."

In both our business and personal lives, we have big rocks, gravel, sand and water. The natural tendency seems to favor the latter three elements, leaving little space for the big rocks. In an effort to respond to the urgent, the important is sometimes set aside.

In your life, you have big rocks, gravel, sand and water. It is easy to fill our pitcher with sand and gravel and then never have room for the big rocks. This happens when we let the little tasks of each day or time wasters fill our pitcher. We end up having to reschedule time for our most important tasks or items because we've already filled our day. The top five priorities you listed earlier could make up most of your big rocks. Gravel could be errands you have to run or small tasks to be accomplished. The sand and water are our "filler" activities and, in some cases, our time wasters.

What I'm going to walk you through next is how to practically set up your schedule with this metaphor in mind. We are going to first block out time for our big rocks, then plan in our gravel or smaller activities and finally, try and leave some time for the filler activities. It takes some work in the beginning to set this up, but it will be so worth it if you follow it. We must set up three types of schedules: daily, weekly and monthly. The first schedule we're going to create is the weekly schedule because it creates the skeleton for how we will schedule everything else. Let's get started.

WEEKLY SCHEDULE

Provided below is an actual class schedule of a college freshman at Baylor University. Let me explain what you'll see on it: her total credit hours are the number of credits she is going to earn this semester. You can look at each of her seven scheduled classes and note that she will be earning anywhere from zero credits, in Chapel, to four credits for her Spanish class. The first line gives the title of the class, the second line gives the number of credits earned, and the third line gives the time and location of the class.

Follow my example in the weekly grid provided below the class schedule and block out class times that are absolutely occupied. We will be going to class, friends! We have to block out those times so we don't plan anything in that time slot during our week.

CLASS SCHEDULE   Total Credit Hours: 16.000

Chapel - CHA 1088 – 05 (TITLE OF CLASS)
Credits: 0.000 (CREDITS EARNED)
Class 11:15 am - 12:05 pm MW Waco Hall (TIME AND LOCATION OF CLASS)

Health & Human Behavior - HED 1145 - 28
Credits: 1.000
Class 1:25 pm - 2:15 pm MW McLean Gymnasium 222

Patterns/Relatnships/Numb Conc - MTH 1315 - 01
Credits: 3.000
Class 9:30 am - 10:45 am TR Sid Richardson Science Bldg 212C

The Christian Scriptures - REL 1310 - 31
Credits: 3.000
Class 12:30 pm - 1:45 pm TR Draper Building 172

Elementary Spanish - SPA 1401 - 11
Credits: 4.000
Class 2:30 pm - 3:20 pm MWF Old Main 122
Class 2:00 pm - 2:50 pm TR Old Main 122

Introduction to Teaching I - TED 1312 - 02
Credits: 3.000
Class 8:00 am - 9:15 am TR Draper Building 215

Theater Appreciation - THEA 1206 - 04
Credits: 2.000
Class 12:20 pm - 1:10 pm MW Hooper-Schaefer Fine Arts Cntr 103

I have blocked out time for Chapel. Now, go through and block out the rest of your classes.

	MON.	TUES.	WED.	THURS.	FRI.	SAT.	SUN.
7:00 AM							
8:00 AM							
9:00 AM							
10:00 AM							
11:00 AM	*chapel*		*chapel*				
12:00 PM							
1:00 PM							
2:00 PM							
3:00 PM							
4:00 PM							
5:00 PM							
6:00 PM							
7:00 PM							
8:00 PM							
9:00 PM							

Now that you've scheduled in your classes, go in and block out time for your priorities including: **time with the Lord, church, study time,** and time for **rest** and **exercise**. Think realistically about when you are most likely going to be able to accomplish these items.

Next, schedule your social activities. Many of these you may not be aware of yet because you haven't figured out what you want to join or even what is available. If you're in that boat, let me give you a couple of sample items to choose from to schedule:

- College Bible Study: Wednesday from 7-8 pm
- On-Campus Ministry Meeting: Monday 8-9 pm
- Sorority Meeting: Tuesday 7-9 pm
- Intramural sports: Thursday 5-8 pm
- Church ministry: Wednesday 6-8 pm

Take a look at our completed weekly schedule. You can probably see the days that are going to be busier than others and the days when you will have more time for leisure activities like hanging out with friends, internet time and going to do fun stuff. This creates your set format for how you will accomplish everything each week. When I got to college, I got out some paper and markers and made a schedule like this for myself. I got a little crazy and even color-coded my activities. I taped this schedule to my desk and referred to it daily as I organized my day and figured out where I was supposed to be.

My challenge for you is that you don't let this schedule we've created stay in this book. When you get to school or sooner if you have your schedule, spend some time creating the set-format for your week. I know it takes a little time to set up, but trust me, it's worth every minute!

MONTHLY SCHEDULE

After creating the format for how everything will be accomplished each week, we can move on to establishing our monthly schedule. To do this you're going to need two things: monthly calendars and your syllabi from your classes. You can go buy a planner or print monthly calendars off of the computer. However, I bet that you will receive several at orientation for free from your school, and you can just use one of them. The second thing you need, your class syllabus, will be given to you the first week of classes free of charge (actually they're quite expensive if you ever look at your tuition payments!). Similar to high school, most college classes will use the first class day to prepare you for the rest of the semester by telling you what you will be doing in their class, what they expect of you and due dates for assignments, projects and tests. Different from high school is that these profs will give you a packet, called a syllabus, that already contains every due date you need to know. Also different from high school, you will likely leave with a major assignment due and a cramped hand from taking notes.

These syllabi, to the surprise of many, are not to be used for a bonfire to help celebrate the start of a new year! They are provided to you to help you plan out your semester and that is exactly how we are going to use them. The syllabus will likely include the class rules, expectations, goals and a course calendar listing all of the assignments and their due dates. So, go back to your dorm room with all of these packets of information, sit down with your monthly calendars and write down when all of your assignments are due. Once you are finished, sit back and look over your work. You will now have a broad picture of what your semester is going to look like. Take a deep breath; you're going to make it!

I want to practice doing this with you. Here is a sample course calendar for The Christian Scriptures class of a college freshman at Baylor. I included the first 7½ weeks of the class. Please take a moment and look over it. This is what the infamous syllabus looks like: you can see that this student takes this class two days a week, Tuesday and Thursday, and that she leaves each class with an assignment to be completed by the next class. In this case, it appears that the majority of the assignments are to read a portion of scripture and a selection from their textbook. This type of class is one in which many students fall behind. Why? Because they think they can put off the reading until test time and then just cram. Don't do it! Inevitably, because you didn't read, you are lost in many of the class discussions and when test time comes you have to learn all of the material instead of just reviewing like the students who kept up along the way. You put yourself at a great disadvantage when you don't stay on top of your assignments.

COURSE CALENDAR

08/26   Introducing the Course: The Christian Grand Narrative

08/28   The Text of the Bible
             Assignment: Harris, 13-25

09/02   The Development of the Christian Canon
             Assignment: Harris, 26-34

09/04   The Beginning of the World
             Assignment: Genesis 1-3; Harris, 40-69

09/09   Grace and Judgment
             Assignment: Genesis 4-11; Harris, 86-108

09/11   The Beginning of a Family
             Assignment: Genesis 12-50; Harris, 108-117

09/16   The Beginning of a Nation: Exodus and Settlement
             Assignment: Exodus 1-24; Joshua 1-7, Harris, 117-133; 147-158

09/18   Test #1

09/23   The Beginning of a Monarchy: Judges, Samuel, and Saul
             Assignment: Judges, 2-8; 13-16; 1 Samuel 1-15; Harris, 158-168

09/25   The United Monarchy: The Reign of David
             Assignment: 1 Samuel 16-31; 2 Samuel 5-12; Harris, 168-173

09/30   The Divided Monarchy: Solomon's Reign and Its Consequences
             Assignment: 1 Kings 1-11, 17-22;Harris, 173-189

10/02   Eighth Century Prophets: Amos and Hosea
             Assignment: Amos 1-6; Hosea 1-5; Harris, 190-201

10/07   Exile and Restoration
             Assignment: 2 Kings 19-25; Ezra, Nehemiah
             Isaiah 40-55; Jeremiah 1-3, 27-31; Ezekiel 1-3, 7, 18, 37; Harris, 201-229

10/09   Worship and Education: Poetry and Wisdom
             Assignment: Psalm 1, 8, 22, 23, 51, 121, 137; Job 1-8; 38-42; Proverbs 1-3; 5-6; 31;
             Ecclesiastes 1-3; Harris, 232-260; 267-283

10/14   Test #2

Now, let's practice what I taught you to do once you receive it. Here's a calendar for just the month of September. Just so that you get a little practice, go through September and fill in all of your assignments and tests for that month.

(Hint: September assignments will be all of those that start with 9/ __)

September

SUNDAY	MONDAY	TUESDAY	WEDNES.	THURSDAY	FRIDAY	SATURDAY
31	1	2	3	4	5	6
7	8	9	10	11	12	13
14	15	16	17	18	19	20
21	22	23	24	25	26	27
28	29	30	1	2	3	4

Way to go! Now you know how to do it so there will be no excuses when it's time to do it for real. You've done a lot so far, and I'm proud of you. This is going to make such an impact on your effectiveness. We're almost done, just one more step in our time management set-up. We need to make the daily schedule.

DAILY SCHEDULE

The final step in our time management process is to create a daily schedule. Either the night before or the morning of the new day, make a list of the things that must be completed that day. Then, reference your weekly schedule to plan when you are going to complete each of those things.

May look like this:
1. Have quiet time
2. Exercise
3. Do two loads of laundry
4. Read Christian Scriptures assignment
5. Read for Elementary Education class
6. Do math assignment
7. Call Mom

Now that you know how and when you are going to accomplish the things the Lord has set before you, you want to make sure that you give your best in all that you do. This leads us to the 7th of our Freshman 15 that we must pack. It is to:

7TH MUST-PACK:
PURSUE EXCELLENCE TO THE END

This must-pack will be accomplished much easier if you are employing the scheduling techniques we just learned about. This is true because I believe that the main reason we don't give 110% in the things we do has a lot to do with procrastination. We tend to put things off that seem overwhelming or not fun and then have to pull an "all-nighter" to get it finished. We end up running in late to class with our pajama pants on and chips that helped get us through the night stuck to our t-shirt. We turn in an essay or project that is nowhere near our best effort. Sure, you hear a lot of people say, "I work best under pressure" and you know what, I've probably said that myself! If that's true for you, set a deadline a few days before the real deadline. Then, set it in your mind that your new date is the *actual* due date. Fake yourself out! This will allow you to edit and perfect it in the days after you are finished.

Our Pursue Excellence to the End must-pack is found in Scripture, so let's take a look at what it has to say:

> Slaves, obey your earthly masters in everything; and do it, not only when their eye is on you and to win their favor, but with sincerity of heart and reverence for the Lord. Whatever you do, work at it with all your heart, as working for the Lord, not for men, since you know that you will receive an inheritance from the Lord as a reward. It is the Lord Christ you are serving (Colossians 3:22-24).

Don't let the "slaves" reference deceive you into thinking that this doesn't apply to you. The Bible Knowledge Commentary explains it like this:

> Principles in Colossians 3:22-25 for Christian slaves may be applied today to Christian employees. If more Christian employees today served their employers with genuine concern and as though they were serving God, quality and productivity would increase dramatically! **It is the Lord Christ** whom all Christians **are serving** (emphasis mine).

During your time in college, your *job* is to be a student. In that sense, your professors become your bosses. The way you behave in class affects your witness. I have found this to be so true in my own life. I saw it from the perspective of a student and then recently, in a whole new way as a teacher. In my last year as a high school Spanish teacher, I had a student who we'll call Kaylee. I must tell you that she was an absolutely wonderful student. She was punctual, attentive, took notes, always turned in homework and actively participated in class. In general, she spoke when asked but was quiet otherwise. I never caught her passing notes, doodling or texting. Kaylee's behavior and effort in my class earned my respect for her. I began to look to her as a "helper" and an example in the classroom. Although I was careful not to show favoritism, I relied on Kaylee for feedback on how well I was explaining a concept or how things had gone with the substitute while I was out.

This young student challenged me, just by her character and actions, to give my best in my classroom. I desired to give her my very best lesson and help her learn all of the Spanish I could. This student was a believer in Christ and demonstrated that in all she did. And, you know what? I know that she wasn't doing it for me! She wasn't all that concerned with my approval. She was serving her Lord and giving Him her best in every class, on every homework assignment and in all that she attempted.

Imagine if I hadn't been a believer or just think of her unbelieving teachers that had seen all of these students that proclaimed to be Christian but just skated by in their classrooms. Now, they were able to see a student that accurately portrayed Christ, not just at FCA meetings or with their friends, but with their teachers and in their schoolwork. Don't be deceived into thinking this doesn't make a difference. It does. By your efforts in your studies, you can prepare a professor or fellow classmate to hear about Christ and you can help tear down the myth of the casual, hypocrite Christian that proclaims Christ with their mouth but denies Him in their actions by running late, cheating and disrespecting the prof by talking and texting.

It may be easy to give your best to your friends, the ministry you're involved in or the sorority you joined, but it is imperative that you also give your best effort in your classes. It is part of the way we represent Christ on our campus and the way that we give glory to God. As it says in 1 Corinthians 10:31, "So whether you eat or drink or whatever you do, do it all for the glory of God."

Part of pursuing excellence means we pursue it to the end. It will be very tempting to just walk through the finish line. I have a tendency to see the end in sight and start to coast. This happens to a lot of students and maybe you've experienced this in high school. The problem is that we all start out the semester gung-ho and excited about having a great year. We are on time to class, turn in all our homework and even study for tests. Then, as the semester wains on, we lose our drive, start to miss class, give half an effort on our assignments and give 2% instead of 100%. Ladies, when we look to Christ, this was not His attitude. Look at his life—He finished strong. We must finish strong each semester, each year and to the end of our lives.

I was particularly interested in the 2008 Summer Olympics. I don't usually get that into it but for some reason, I watched it almost from beginning to end. The opening ceremonies in Bejing were breath-taking and the athleticism that the gymnasts and swimmers displayed was record-breaking. Toward the end of the Olympics came the track and field events. Everyone was talking about the Jamaican team, especially a young man named Usain Bolt. It was as if he had been prepared from birth because of his last name to run like, well…a lightning bolt! My husband and I watched in great anticipation as he ran the 100 meter race and couldn't believe our eyes when we saw how he finished the race. Here's an article about Bolt's efforts:

The Sunday Times

August 17, 2008

9.69—and Usain Bolt didn't even break sweat

Time stood still in the Birds Nest last night. The clock at first registered 9.68sec just as Usain Bolt was hurtling across the finishing line and heading with jet-propelled shoes towards the stands on the far side of the track. When it was adjusted to a mere 9.69sec, in the interests of modesty, 91,000 people still rubbed their eyes in astonishment not just at the new world record time but at the fact that the new Olympic champion was showboating 10m before the finish. Had he pulled out all the stops, the clock would have cried out for mercy (Andrew Longmore).

What he accomplished was incredible, but tragically, he stopped trying long before the race was over. He merely sauntered through the finish line. He put the brakes on and coasted in, taking in all of his glory before he received the reward. I remember my husband and I looking at each other with jaws dropped in amazement and just shook our heads at what could have just happened. This man could have completely crushed the record books but chose to coast instead.

Ladies, don't let this be true of you. You don't ever want to look back on a single semester and think of what *could have* happened. My challenge to you is that you finish strong.
Paul, our example of a single-focused life, was able to say near the end of his time on earth:

> I have fought the good fight, I have finished the race, I have kept the faith. Now there is in store for me the crown of righteousness, which the Lord, the righteous Judge, will award to me on that day—and not only to me, but also to all who have longed for his appearing (2 Timothy 4:6-8).

Don't you desire to be able to say the same? I know I do. My final exhortation about purposing your life to glorify God comes from Hebrews 12:1-3:

> Therefore, since we are surrounded by such a great cloud of witnesses, let us throw off everything that hinders and the sin that so easily entangles, and let us run with perseverance the race marked out for us. Let us fix our eyes on Jesus, the author and perfecter of our faith, who for the joy set before him endured the cross, scorning its shame, and sat down at the right hand of the throne of God. Consider him who endured such opposition from sinful men, so that you will not grow weary and lose heart.

Throw off the things that are keeping you from running straight for your heavenly calling. Remember that Rick Warren told us "to prune away even the good activities and do only what matters most."

We packed four more items into our suitcase in this chapter. Can you list them? Look back in the chapter if you need a little help jogging your memory and then fill in the blanks below:

4TH MUST-PACK:_____

5TH MUST-PACK:_____

6TH MUST-PACK:_____

7TH MUST-PACK:_____

Which of these do you think will be the easiest for you to take with you to college?

Which of these do you think will be the hardest to implement?

As we end this chapter, we are almost to the halfway point of completing our Freshman 15. I want you to know that I'm proud of the work you've done so far and am so thankful for ladies like you— ladies who see the importance in preparing for college and doing what they need to do to use their college years to influence the Kingdom. I'm praying for you as you let all of these lessons soak into your minds and hearts.

Speaking of hearts, in our next chapter we're going to tackle some issues that most likely affect our hearts more than the other chapters in this study: Dudes and Dating. So take a breather, meditate on what you've learned, and when you're ready…

DUDES AND DATING

When you go to register for college, you will have to choose which class track to take based on the type of degree you want. Your primary choices will be either a BA (Bachelor of Arts) or a BS (Bachelor of Science). Some girls, however, will go in scouring their university's programs looking for a whole other type of degree. They want their MRS! Their dream is to walk off the graduation stage and down the wedding aisle. I hate to break it to you, in case you're one of those girls, but you won't find it in the university catalog. Trust me; I looked when I was aiming to get mine.

Some ladies are so determined to graduate from college with their MRS that they involve themselves in all kinds of scheming to make sure they get it. Some aren't doing it out of desperation. They've just assumed that the plan for their life was to go to college, meet their future mate, graduate, get married and have kids. This certainly is not a bad plan but it's not the *only* plan. When you confine God's timing to those four years (or five or six for some of you), you are limiting God's best for your life. Let me explain.

Instead of asking the Lord which church to attend and what activities to get involved in, you're researching where the best guys are to help make your decision. Instead of going on mission trips or taking summers to work at a camp or interning at a church, you worry if that will isolate you too much from available men. You can get so focused on trying to meet "the one" that you miss out on getting to know "The Only One".

I know because I went through a period in my college years in which I was singularly focused on finding "the one". I believed *he* was at my school — it was just a matter of meeting. I didn't want to limit where God would have us meet, so I was always on the lookout. I would ride the elevator with a cute guy that smiled at me and think, "Is he the one?" I'd sit next to a guy in class who asked to borrow a pencil and think, "Is he the one?" My roommate would bring a new friend over to the house and I'd instantly think, "Could he be the one?" before I even knew his name! As a former MRS seeker, I implore you to not waste your time in this pursuit. The Lord cares for you deeply and is taking care of this issue. Trust Him!

Thankfully, the Lord got a hold of me and shook all of that ridiculousness out of my heart and mind.

My dear, older sister gave me a book that I highly recommend called *Lady in Waiting*. It helped focus my eyes back on the most important man in my life, Jesus Christ. I remember reading the convicting statement that it is, "not about finding the right man, but being the right woman" (*Lady in Waiting*, preface). I re-focused my energies on being all that God was calling me to be. I committed to stop wasting time in college consumed with my singleness. I was able to start trusting God with my heart and my future instead of trying to take matters into my own hands.

We are fortunate to have a biblical example of a woman that was able to trust God with her heart. Her name is Ruth. Her trip didn't take her to college, but to Bethlehem. Like you will be doing, she had to leave all that was familiar to her and go where she believed would honor God.

Here's Ruth's story:

> In the days when the judges ruled, there was a famine in the land, and a man from Bethlehem in Judah, together with his wife and two sons, went to live for a while in the country of Moab. The man's name was Elimelech, his wife's name Naomi, and the names of his two sons were Mahlon and Kilion. They were Ephrathites from Bethlehem, Judah. And they went to Moab and lived there.

> Now Elimelech, Naomi's husband, died, and she was left with her two sons. They married Moabite women, one named Orpah and the other Ruth. After they had lived there about ten years, both Mahlon and Kilion also died, and Naomi was left without her two sons and her husband. When she heard in Moab that the LORD had come to the aid of his people by providing food for them, Naomi and her daughters-in-law prepared to return home from there.

> With her two daughters-in-law she left the place where she had been living and set out on the road that would take them back to the land of Judah. Then Naomi said to her two daughters-in-law, "Go back, each of you, to your mother's home. May the LORD show kindness to you, as you have shown to your dead and to me. May the LORD grant that each of you will find rest in the home of another husband."...

> But Ruth replied, "Don't urge me to leave you or to turn back from you. Where you go I will go, and where you stay I will stay. Your people will be my people and your God my God. Where you die I will die, and there I will be buried. May the LORD deal with me, be it ever so severely, if anything but death separates you and me." When Naomi realized that Ruth was determined to go with her, she stopped urging her (Ruth 1:1-9, 16-18).

Where was Ruth from? (circle one)   MOAB   or   BETHLEHEM

Where was her husband from? (circle one)   MOAB   or   BETHLEHEM

What happened to her husband?

Where was Naomi going?

Why did Naomi want Ruth and Orpah to go back to their mother's home in Moab?

Why do you think Ruth "was determined to go with her"?

Ruth, now widowed, believed that she was to follow Naomi even though she realized it most likely meant she would never re-marry and never bear children. The Bible Knowledge Commentary describes her decision this way:

> But she chose life with Naomi over her family, her national identity, and her religious idolatry. In one of the most beautiful expressions of commitment in all the world's literature she laced her future to that of Naomi. She confessed allegiance to the people of Israel and to the God of Israel. Here was a stirring example of a complete break with the past. Like Abraham Ruth decided to leave her ancestors' idolatrous land to go to the land of promise. And Ruth did it without the encouragement of a promise. In fact she made her decision despite Naomi's strenuous encouragement to do otherwise.

In Ruth's time, marriage meant security. If she wanted to make sure that she was taken care of by finding a husband, her chances would have been much better if she would have stayed in Moab. However, she was giving all that she trusted in and all of her hope for security over to the Lord. She trusted Him to take care of her every need as she followed Him. What follows is a wonderful love story between Ruth and the man God sent to care for her, Boaz. God's ideal for Ruth was infinitely better than what Naomi thought she needed. God sent a kinsman redeemer to marry Ruth, love her and take care of her and Naomi. I hope you are able to follow Ruth's example and believe that when you follow God with your whole heart, He will take care of you.

When we truly trust the Lord, like Ruth did, we let go and let God. Giving all of our hopes, dreams, emotions and longings to the Lord puts them in the right place. He can be trusted with them. Doing that, turning your heart over to Him, is how we pack our 8th item into our Freshman 15 suitcase.

8TH  MUST-PACK:
GUARD YOUR HEART

As I mentioned before, we can trust God to protect our hearts. Do you believe that, really? Or, do you think that you might need to take matters into your own hands if He doesn't bring the right guy along?

As honestly as you can, rank yourself on this trust scale by circling the line that represents you:

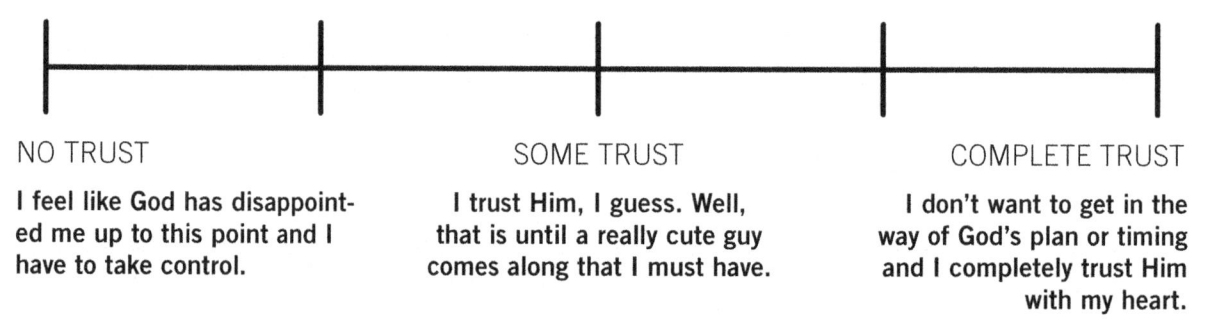

NO TRUST	SOME TRUST	COMPLETE TRUST
I feel like God has disappointed me up to this point and I have to take control.	I trust Him, I guess. Well, that is until a really cute guy comes along that I must have.	I don't want to get in the way of God's plan or timing and I completely trust Him with my heart.

I hope you were able to circle COMPLETE TRUST. I want you to put your heart in His hands and turn it over to Him as you trust Him to give you all you need. Ladies, He knows what you need and will take care of you. Psalm 37:4 promises, "Delight yourself in the Lord and he will give you the desires of your heart."

This must-pack to guard your heart comes from Philippians 4:6-7, "Do not be anxious about anything, but in everything, by prayer and petition, with thanksgiving, present your requests to God. And the peace of God, which transcends all understanding, will guard your hearts and your minds in Christ Jesus." (emphasis mine). We guard our hearts by being honest with God about our thoughts, emotions and hopes and presenting them to Him. As a symbolic gesture of your willingness to put your complete trust in Him, please take a moment to pray this prayer below and then draw a heart within the open hands on the page. They represent the hands of our Lord who is ready to take your heart in them and keep it safe. Please pray:

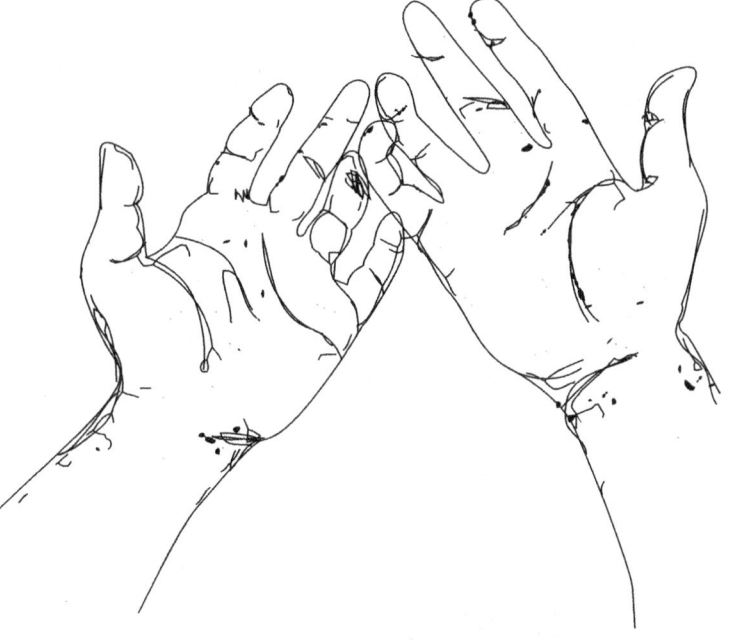

Loving God,

I believe you when you tell me that you know the plans You have for me. I believe that You are giving me Your best. I surrender to You my desire to take control over my heart and my life. I offer to You all of me. I give over all of my dreams for a husband and what I want out of dating. Here is my heart. I trust you to take care of it.

Symbolically, place your heart in His hands by drawing a heart within the open hands.

His hands are the only safe place for our hearts. The way we keep our heart safe, which includes all of our desire to be romanced, is by letting the Lord take over it. He wants you to seek out the Greatest Romance, which is found in knowing Him. Instead of spending your college time searching after Mr. Right, guard your heart by seeking after the Ultimate Mr. Right, our Heavenly Bridegroom, Jesus Christ.

Have you ever heard Christ called the Bridegroom? The term is used many times throughout scripture to describe the love relationship between Christ and the church. The church, which includes you, is the bride of Christ and He is your Bridegroom. One day, the Great Wedding will take place when He returns for His church. Isn't it wonderful that Christ would choose such an intimate metaphor to describe His love toward His people?

Ephesians 5:25-27 talks about this love relationship:

> ...just as Christ loved the church and gave himself up for her to make her holy, cleansing her by the washing with water through the word, and to present her to himself as a radiant church, without stain or wrinkle or any other blemish, but holy and blameless.

I am amazed at the way He cares for me, cleanses me and desires to know me. I belong to my Bridegroom (John 3:28) and am amazed that "as a bridegroom rejoices over his bride, so will your God rejoice over you" (Isaiah 62:5b). He loves you tenderly and deeply with the best, perfect love.

He desires to know you more and to have an intimate relationship with you. He wants to talk to you, hear about your day and how you're feeling. He wants you to read His letters to you and communicate how much He loves you. This is the man that showed the ultimate expression of love, He gave His life for you. Zephaniah 3:17 tells us that, "The Lord your God is with you, he is mighty to save. He will take great delight in you, he will quiet you with his love, he will rejoice over you with singing." How amazing that the God of the Universe is rejoicing over me with singing and that He takes delight in me!

I have to admit that when someone explained this concept to me, that Christ was in love with me, I was a little uneasy about it. I had always thought of Jesus as a man dressed in a robe and sandals that went around teaching, healing and baptizing. Don't get me wrong, I thought He was amazing, but my thoughts and ideals of Him were so distant. I didn't realize that I could have a love relationship with Him, so that when I heard His name it meant so much more. He changed from Jesus, the distant teacher, to Jesus, Lover of my soul.

I truly fell in love with the Lord in a whole new way and poured my heart out to Him. Here are a few excerpts from my journal during this time:

8/6/01
Lord God, my heart is fragile and easily broken when I hold it—however, I know that it is safe in Your hands. I ask for You to take control of my heart...I desire to reflect You in my purity. I am so in love with You and I desire to fall so much more in love with You...

8/10/01
God in Heaven, thank You for being so much more than that. You love me so much that You couldn't leave the relationship as simply God in Heaven. You became God on earth and God that resides in me. I am undeserving of such a privilege.

8/24/01
The Lover of my Soul, Thank You for recklessly and relentlessly pursuing me. Even when I give my affections to other "lovers"—You still chase after me.

9/3/01
Redeemer, I rejoice this morning because You live! You are awesome and so wonderful my God and King. Thank You for waking me this morning with renewed strength.

10/13/01
Thank You for this wonderful, beautiful, crisp day. I love the cold air and the sweet breeze. Thank You for a quiet day to rest, relax and get refreshed...I desire to fall more in love with You, Lord. I pray that You would open my eyes to the amazing ways You are romancing me.

I challenge you to "date" Jesus before you date anyone else. Treat your time with Him like a dating relationship. Write Him letters, talk to Him, spend time reading what He has written to you in His Word. This dating time with Jesus will prepare your heart and teach you how to date guys correctly, not like the world does. We have a much loftier and more wonderful romance available to us. Christ desires to teach you what that looks like.

A dear friend of mine blessed me with a letter from Jesus to us that I have cherished. Now, it is soft and worn down from the many times I have read it. I pulled it out during my dating years to draw near to the Truth of what God was saying to me. I want to share a part of the letter with you and hope that it speaks to your heart the way it spoke to mine.

> Beloved,
>
> I cherish you. I shed My blood so that you could be clean. I want you for My companion, My bride, to love and to cherish now and throughout eternity and I plan to dress you in the most beautiful of white garments. As you live out the joy and experience the wonder of being My bride, I will be your gentle tutor conforming you to My image. I must begin by teaching you how to serve and live in submission to me. Let me convince you of your great value and that intimacy is ever so much more than sex. Then, when you are healed, you will be able to fully share the love I have given you with the one you someday choose to bring to Me as your earthly husband. Then, and only then, will you be the kind of wife I would choose for him. Give yourself completely to Me. I want you to deny Me nothing. I will not hurt you. I will not disappoint you. You can trust Me—completely. I keep My promises.
>
> Love,
>
> Jesus

My hope is that you would know Christ the way I came to know Him. That you would fall in love with Him and allow a love relationship with Him to be all you need. I agree with Joshua Harris when he says, "Before two people can please God as a couple, they must first be individuals who want God more than anything else and who know that only He can satisfy the deepest longings of their souls" (*Boy Meets Girl*). This, ladies, is how we keep our hearts safely guarded in God's hands, by giving Him our hearts, trusting Him with our every desire and finding completeness in knowing Him alone.

How do we guard our hearts? Circle all that apply:

Scheming to get the guys we want   Putting our hearts in the Lord's hands

    Dating Jesus   Researching where the most available hotties hang out

Coming to God with all of our hopes and dreams   Giving all of ourselves over to a guy

Now that you have your heart resting safely in the Lords' hands, you are ready to consider what kind of guys you will date. Be careful as you begin to date that you don't try and take control again over your heart. The only place we can trust it is in God's hands; He'll keep it safe for you until your wedding day.

Are you ready for the next must-pack? As we are trusting God with our heart, guys will undoubtedly still come into the picture. You will probably be asked out on dates by some of them. What should you keep in mind as you accept dates? How about the next must-pack…

9TH 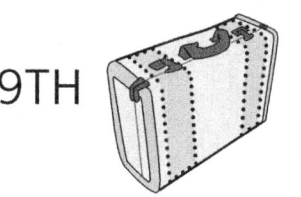 MUST-PACK: EVERY DATE IS A POTENTIAL MATE

I found this statement in *Lady in Waiting* and remember thinking how simple and obvious it was, yet forgotten by too many of us. Think about it, it all starts with one date. You will start the romantic relationship with the man you will eventually marry on a single date. Obvious, right? I hope so. I hope it is so obvious that you realize that you shouldn't waste your time dating guys you know you would never marry. There are so many pitfalls to this type of dating. The biggest one is that you may not be able to tear yourself away from the guy and end up with him for years, knowing the whole time that he was not good for you. Trust me, I've seen it happen too many times. Girls get desperate and say "yes" to whoever asks them out and then months or years later they are devastated because he finally broke off what never should have begun in the first place.

What are some other pitfalls to dating guys you know don't live up to your standards:

Please, don't settle for Mr. Right Now! Don't waste your time on guys that you know you wouldn't want to marry. Let's talk about a few of the obvious character traits or problems that you want to be on the lookout for.

First, scripture very clearly instructs believers not to be "bound together" with non-believers (2 Corinthians 6:14). This does not mean that you are not to associate with non-believers, of course that would not be true. However, you do not want to partner with someone who cannot understand the deepest part of who you are, and you do not want to risk falling away from the Lord because of the influence of your boyfriend.

Let me put it bluntly: you are NOT to date non-believers. This includes you ladies who want to save a guy and therefore attempt what we like to call "Missionary Dating." Girls justify it by saying, "Oh, he's so sweet. I just know that if he came to know Jesus he'd be perfect." Well, that may be true but it's not your job to save him, and it is very dangerous to attempt to witness to someone by dating them! We aren't here to bring guys to Christ over candlelit dinners. If he's not a Christian, you should not be dating him. It will save you from tremendous pain and disappointment. Do not accept dates from non-believers.

You should also be aware of certain character traits that don't necessarily demonstrate the heart of a growing Christian. A few of these sinful characteristics the Bible warns against are: selfishness, anger, verbal and physical abuse, lack of ambition, and substance abuse or addiction.

These negative attributes are all things that the Lord can work out in a Christ follower. However, you have to let the Lord do His work. If you see one of these sin areas starting to rear its ugly head, step away from the guy so that God can get in there and work. Frankly, if you are struggling with any of those sins, you may need to take a break from dating and allow the Refiner to do some work in you.

I want to warn you that sinful habits that bother you at the beginning only get more irritating and difficult to handle as you go. Marriage not only puts a ring on your finger, but it also puts a huge spotlight on the worst aspects of who you are. If there is something about a guy you are dating that you know you couldn't deal with, get outta there! Marrying him won't fix it. If he's lazy and lacks ambition, he is probably not going to come home from the honeymoon and go out and conquer the world. More than likely, he will go back to conquering his place on the couch. My husband always counsels with this advice: "If you want to change your partner, change partners." If there is a major character flaw, don't expect to be able to change it down the road. "You want to marry someone for the qualities he possesses now, not the qualities you hope he will develop" (*Lady in Waiting*, p. 154).

I am thankful to have had the dating experiences that I have so that I can empathize with what you are going through. As I said before, I eventually learned to put my heart in God's hands but before that, I made a few dating mishaps. I have learned what it is like to date the wrong kind of guy the wrong way and the right kind of guy the right way. Let's start with the wrong kind of guy, the wrong way.

My freshman year of college, I met this super hot guy, Chris, at a party. First of all, let me say I shouldn't have been at the party in the first place. The road it started me down was a rocky one. But anyway, back to the story...So I met this guy and when he introduced himself to me, I felt weak in the knees. He was what the world considers very good-looking; I even learned later that he had done some modeling. All of the girls at the party were interested in him. He seemed to like me when we talked for those few minutes but then appeared aloof and uninterested the rest of the night. I remember this "got to have him" feeling coming over me. Why do we do that as girls? Why do we have this desire to chase after the un-gettable guy? I know it was sin within me.

I fell into that sinful, scheming trap and set in my mind that I would *make* him want me. A little conniving on my part, and in no time, he was calling me up and asking me out. We went out several times and hung out over at his apartment a lot. Somewhere in the back of my mind, I knew I shouldn't be with him. Actually, it was brought to the forefront of my mind when he began his pursuit of me sexually. I don't know how we got to that point without me realizing because the signs were obvious.

First, he said he was a Christian, but I knew that his lifestyle did not reflect it whatsoever. Second, he was so focused on himself and what he wanted that he treated others, including his friends and roommates, badly. Third, he wasn't interested in getting to know me and about me. I discovered later that he was more interested in "knowing" my body than who I was as a person. I think something triggered in him when I told him that I was a virgin and was not going to have sex until I was married. It's like it set off this desire to conquer me—to break me down until I gave away to him what I so desperately only wanted to give to my husband.

He was crafty, too, and I was naïve. One of my favorite examples of his maneuvering came the first time he tried to get me to stay the night. It was late and we had all been watching movies at his apartment. Everyone had left and it was dark and cold outside. So he said, "You know you could just stay over. I saw this *Saved by the Bell* episode one time where the girl slept under the covers and the guy slept on top of them so that they weren't touching. We could do that so you wouldn't feel bad about it." Wow! Really?!? *Saved by the Bell?* Now, I can look back at that and laugh knowing how ridiculous it sounds, but at the time, I must shamefully say that I fell for it hook, line and sinker. After that point, he kept eroding away at my convictions. He would tell me over and over how "not a big deal" it was to have sex — how everyone was doing it. He even tried to tell me he was falling in love with me! That last one finally shocked me into reality. I realized that he was trying the oldest tricks in the book to get me to go to bed with him and I finally gave him the boot. It was tough though and I wish, looking back, that I would have never even started down that path. You know what the end result was for me? I had less of myself to give only to my husband. Little parts of me and my heart were left there in that apartment. I knew going into it that this guy had no "potential mate" qualities that I was looking for, but I went out with him anyway. He may have been a Christian, but he definitely didn't have signs of a growing relationship with Christ and he had so many un-surrendered sinful habits. Bottom line: wrong kind of guy, the wrong way.

The same year, I met another guy at a dorm mixer. His name was Justin, and he was friends with a guy I knew from student government. Do you know what we talked about the night we met? Church. He wanted to hear all about my ministry with the youth and all about my church. The next time I ran into him was at my church. He brought his sister and her roommates that also went to our school. For a while, that was the only time I saw him. Then, he told me that he would love to help with the youth group, too, and would I mind if he asked the youth pastor if he could get on our team? He actually asked me! Of course I told him that I thought it was a great idea. Soon, Justin was an active part of the youth ministry. We mostly got to know each other through serving together. Honestly, I didn't even realize that he had any romantic feelings for me for a few months. During that time of getting to know each other, he was always a gentleman and completely unselfish. He always opened my doors, really listened to me when I talked and was interested in how he could help me. Then, I came down with a bad cold and he brought me soup. I saw his servant's heart, his deep love relationship with the Lord and realized that this was a guy I wanted to get to know better. Right after that, he sat me down and we had our first DTR (define the relationship). He told me that he would like to take me on a date and see what God had for both of us. You know, I didn't end up marrying him but I am so thankful for the time I had to date him. He was a guy that guarded my heart by not playing with my emotions, was pure in his motives toward me and when we departed, I was stronger spiritually. Bottom line: right kind of guy, the right way.

After that, I fervently pursued a love relationship with my Jesus. I sought to fall in love with only Him. I grew so much spiritually and see that time in my life as a wonderful, sold-out romance with my Savior. The Lord kept my heart safe in His very capable hands until He brought me the love of my life, my husband, Jeremy.

I actually met Jeremy when I was in high school and he was working as a college intern for our youth group. I must say that I was smitten with him immediately! At 15, Jeremy "set the bar" for what I was looking for in a man. His love relationship with the Lord was inspiring. He loved others, served with such joy and was so fun to be around. He made me laugh and I loved listening to him teach the youth group. I knew in my heart that a relationship between us wasn't God's will at the time and willingly gave over my desire for Jeremy. He graduated from college and left town. Years went by and I would think of him but assumed that the Lord had closed the door there. Out of the blue, as far as I could tell, he called me up one day and told me that I had been on his heart and he wanted to know how I was doing. We chatted off and on for a few weeks and then I left for my freshman year of college. He would write me encouraging letters and ask me five getting-to-know-you questions at the end of each. He sent worship CDs from bands he knew I liked and called infrequently to see how I was doing. Jeremy showed such a pure heart in the way he sought to really get to know me and encourage my walk.

When I returned home to do my sophomore year at Texas A&M University, he came to town to go to a football game with me. That weekend, the Lord opened my eyes to what He had been orchestrating all this time. I realized that this man that I had met so many years ago might actually be the man

I was supposed to marry. The romance continued to unfold and we each continually laid it at the feet of our Savior. Then, Jeremy called me and told me to pack my bags for cold weather because he was coming to get me the next morning for a road trip. Our final destination: Aspen, Colorado. Jeremy proposed to me on the porch of a hilltop chapel. Of course, I said "Yes!" and we cried and prayed together on that porch, committing our relationship forever to the Lord. I am daily blessed to be married to such a wonderful man. I am so thankful that my journey didn't end with the first guy I dated in college. I can't imagine how miserable I would be. Instead, He sent me a man that is more wonderful than I could have ever imagined for myself. It took that time of just Jesus and me to get my heart right so that I was ready to love Jeremy.

We've talked about the wrong kind of guy and the damage it caused and how wonderful it can be with the right kind of guy. Let's look, specifically, at qualities you should be looking for in guys you accept dates from. You're not going to find "talk, dark and handsome" or "blonde hair, blue eyes" in my suggestions. These are deeper, spiritually significant qualities. Trust the Lord to take care of the physical attraction. Don't let that be your litmus test of whether the guy would be good to date—you saw where it got me with Chris. Instead, ask the Lord what kind of man He would have you date. When I prayed over this many years ago, the Lord brought qualities to mind that were specific to me and ones that I added to my list from *Lady in Waiting* because I believed they were vital. They are all based in scripture.

Here are the qualities from *Lady in Waiting*:
- Puts the needs of others ahead of his own (Philippians 2:3-4)
- Rejoices in his relationship with Christ (John 15:11)
- Maintains proper relationships (Hebrews 12:14)
- Refuses to jump ahead of God's timing (Psalm 37:7)
- Understands the importance of feelings and emotions (Colossians 3:12)
- Flees the temptation to compromise (Proverbs 25:28)

Here are a few from my list:
- Growing relationship with the Lord (Hebrews 5:11-14)
- Actively involved in church (Ephesians 4:12)
- Leads me spiritually (Ephesians 5:25-27)
- Treasures me as a princess of the King (Ephesians 5:28-29)

Do any of these qualities stand out to you as ones you would like to have on your list? Can you think of any you'd like to add? List at least five qualities that you want in guys you date:
(A scripture reference is helpful to make sure that it is biblically and not worldly based.)

1. _____

2. _____

3. _____

4. _____

5. _____

When you accept a date from the right kind of guy, the "potential mate" type, you want to honor God with that relationship. Remember, the purpose of your life, which includes dating, is to glorify God. Joshua Harris in *Boy Meets Girl* explains, "I believe that getting our romantic relationships right as Christians means seeing God's glory as the ultimate purpose of any relationship." That means placing that relationship on the altar, and like we did with our hearts, putting it in the Lord's care. We must ask God to help us serve Him in our dating relationships. Practically, we will seek to serve the other person, keep their best in mind, keep them pure and encourage them spiritually. How wonderful dating can be when you are both in pursuit of God's glory. Seek this type of dating: God's glory dating with the right kind of guy, the right way. God will be glorified and your heart will be kept safe.

Keep the qualities we talked about in mind as you accept dates, and don't settle. God has an amazing romance waiting for you, but your first romance must be with only Him. When you are ready, if that is His plan for you, He will send you an earthly mate. In your service to Him, by ffering Him your heart and relationships, He is glorified and pleased with you.

A part of dating for God's glory means that we follow His instructions to stay pure. That's why we must go ahead and pack our next item.

10TH  MUST-PACK: PROTECT YOUR PURITY

Let me warn you: We are about to talk about SEX. Yes, that's right, SEX. If it makes you uncomfortable or a little squeamish, then it's time to put on your big girl pants and deal with it! Because, let's face it, everyone else is talking about it. Magazines, TV, friends at school, billboards, all scream out their opinions. The voice that seems to get lost in the discussion is the church. Right here and now, we are going to tackle the issue with some pretty frank discussion. Take a moment and ask the Lord to clear your mind and thoughts of all of the false things the world has taught you about sex. Ask him to prepare your heart and mind to hear what He has to say about it from His Word. Let Him know that you desire to serve Him in the sexual part of your being.

Here is some space for you to write out your prayer, if you would like:

Did you cringe when I told you to talk to the Lord about the sexual part of you? Let me make this very clear, YOU SHOULDN'T! What has happened in our Christian circles is that we've so outlawed sex that we don't even feel comfortable talking to the Lord about it. We've been told, "NO! NO! NO!" for so long that we've decided it surely must be something that God detests and finds dirty. Ladies, God invented sex! Do you realize that? He made you with your *specific physical makeup* and he made men with their *specific physical makeup*. It wasn't a mistake. He knew what He was doing and what He intended to be done with that *specific physical makeup*! We need to be talking about this with Him, the Creator of everything sexual within you. He is the only One who knows how to correctly handle the equipment for its best good. Remember, He created it!

I love what Al Mohler says about this:

> Christians have no right to be embarrassed when it comes to talking about sex and sexuality. An unhealthy reticence or embarrassment in dealing with these issues is a form of disrespect to God's creation. Whatever God made is good, and every good thing God made has an intended purpose that ultimately reveals His own glory. When conservative Christians respond to sex with ambivalence or embarrassment, we slander the goodness of God and hide God's glory which is intended to be revealed in the right use of creation's gifts (Al Mohler from *Sex and the Supremacy of Christ*, p. 14 by John Piper and Justin Taylor).

John Piper is another man who has something to say on the subject. In Piper's wonderful book *Desiring God*, he teaches that, "God is most glorified in us when we are most satisfied in Him." Piper carries this concept to the sexual arena by saying, "The gigantic secret of the joy of sex is this: *Sex is good because the God who created sex is good. And God is glorified greatly when we receive his gift with thanksgiving and enjoy it the way he meant for it to be enjoyed*" (John Piper, *Sex and the Supremacy of Christ*, p. 55). Do you realize that God could have made sex as a boring, unsatisfactory transaction between two people in order to procreate? Instead, married believers are offered an exhilarating, sensual experience to delight in God's goodness and give Him glory through their sexual intimacy.

> God intends for us to experience tremendous joy and satisfaction in our sexual relationship with our husbands. And what greater proof do we need than the fact that God included the Song of Solomon in Holy Scripture—an entire book of the Bible devoted to love, romance and sexuality in marriage... This little book portrays a physical relationship between husband and wife that is filled with uninhibited passion and exhilarating delight. This is God's heart and aim for our sexual experience. We are to receive sex as a wonderful gift from him and enjoy it for his glory (Carolyn Mahaney, *Sex and the Supremacy of Christ*, p. 202).

You may be asking yourself, "Why is she giving me all of this information on why sex is so great and then telling me not to get near it until I'm married?" Good question! My answer is two-fold. First, I want you to see sex in the proper light, in the light of God's glory in creation. As a way to help me abstain from sex, many well-meaning Christians taught me that sex was wrong and dirty. I allowed those thoughts to penetrate my mind to such an extent that when I entered into marriage and was told that I could now enjoy sex, it was hard to turn off the old message. I had to do a lot of studying, communicating with my husband and talking with the Lord in order to untangle the mess I had made of sex. I want to save you from that heartache. Second, the anticipation of such an amazing act is part of the preciousness of it.

Think of your purity like a gift. Have you ever seen a big box with beautiful wrapping sitting around the Christmas tree and when you went to look closer you realized it was addressed to you? Suddenly, your eyes get big, your heart starts to pound and you get excited about the day you get to open that gift and find the wonderful treasure inside. What would happen to all of that enthusiasm on Christmas morning if, instead of waiting, you had secretly unwrapped the present to see what was inside? So much of the excitement of unwrapping that present was sucked out when you opened it too early. What about your parents, who gave you the gift? What if they knew you peeked? Their joy too would be deflated. Now, think about your wedding day instead of Christmas morning. Part of the anticipation of that wonderful night is this gift you've been storing up that you *finally* get to open. A huge part of the gift is that it is sacred, untouched and anticipated with great joy for you and the only one you choose to share it with. You need to know that sex between a married couple is meant to be beautiful, wonderful and enjoyed. You also need to know that the hope of all you are going to experience is part of what makes it so incredible.

The Lord desires to save this physical intimacy for a husband and wife so that like Mohler said, God's glory is revealed "...in the *right use* of creation's gifts" (italics mine). He calls us to save sharing our *whole selves* with someone until marriage and to honor Him with our purity: "It is God's will that you should be sanctified: that you should avoid sexual immorality; that each of you should learn to control his own body in a way that is holy and honorable, not in passionate lust like the heathen, who do not know God; ...For God did not call us to be impure, but to live a holy life" (1 Thessalonians 4:3-5,7). Scripture makes it very clear that God prohibits sexual immorality, which occurs when we have sex outside of marriage. 1 Corinthians 6:13b verifies this truth, "The body is not meant for sexual immorality, but for the Lord, and the Lord for the body." Randy Alcorn adds, "He expects His children to live a life of purity, a plan that is designed not only for His glory but for our benefit" (Randy Alcorn, *The Purity Principle*, p.5).

The Enemy wants to deceive you by making you think that God is power-hungry and withholding something good from you in order to hurt you. Remember the story of Eve in the Garden of Eden. The devil, disguised as a serpent, found Eve and very cunningly tried to turn God's words around to make her think she was missing out on something. The conversation went like this:

> Now the serpent was more crafty than any of the wild animals the LORD God had made. He said to the woman, "Did God really say, 'You must not eat from any tree in the garden'?"
>
> The woman said to the serpent, "We may eat fruit from the trees in the garden, but God did say, 'You must not eat fruit from the tree that is in the middle of the garden, and you must not touch it, or you will die.'"
>
> "You will not surely die," the serpent said to the woman. "For God knows that when you eat of it your eyes will be opened, and you will be like God, knowing good and evil." (Genesis 3:1-4)

Did you see what the serpent did there? He just barely changed God's words and lied to Eve to make her think that she had somehow been duped by her Creator. He tried to make it seem like he was helping her out but he certainly was not. He is a liar and the father of lies (John 8:44), and his mission is not to help us in any way but instead to steal, kill and destroy (John 10:10).

Do you know what happens next? This is the story of the fall of man. The terrible consequences of this one decision were that man would be separated from the Lord because of sin. You and I will not experience the relationship with God that Adam and Eve had before the fall until we reach our Heavenly home. Wow! It was one little lie, one little serpent, lots of damage. That's how it happens, ladies. Don't be deceived into thinking that Satan is going to come out in a big red suit with horns and a stick and tell you to do something ridiculous you know you shouldn't. Obviously, you'd be like, "Oh, you're Satan. I've seen drawings of you before and I've seen you in cartoons. I'm definitely not going to do what you say." That would be way too easy. Instead, he makes a little twist in God's Word, puts a little thought in your head, helps you justify one little action and then... lots of damage.

Picture this. You started a relationship saying you weren't going to kiss, now, you're alone together, it's dark and you want to so bad. You hear the little lie that says, "Go ahead. It's just a kiss. It's no big deal. Forget about your 'boundaries'. You're probably gonna marry this guy anyway." So, you kiss. What's the big deal? The big deal may be that you continue to justify your physical intimacy until you finally give away all of yourself to this guy. We'll talk more about the potential damage but let me start with a few consequences, such as heartbreak, pregnancy and STDs. It was one little justification, one little kiss that Satan used to damage you. He is very clever in his schemes and will do all that he can to tempt you and wear you down. Let me tell you a little about the two ways Satan's temptation tactics work. Often, he'll try to tempt you when your defenses are down and you are weak or when you are feeling so good that you would never expect it.

We'll take the example of when Jesus was tempted in the desert three times. This story takes place in Luke 4:1-13, immediately after Jesus had just been baptized in Luke 3. Satan tempts Jesus three times, each time trying to distort scripture to serve his own evil purposes and convince Jesus that he is right. First, Jesus is hungry from fasting and Satan tempts him to turn stones to bread. Christ refuses with scripture. Second, Satan tempts Jesus to jump off a high point because the angels will catch Him. Christ refuses with scripture. Third, Satan took Jesus to a high mountain and told Jesus that he would give Him control over everything if only Jesus would bow and worship Satan. Christ refuses with scripture. Then, in Luke 4:13 it says, "When the devil had finished all this tempting, he left him until an opportune time."

Jesus was leaving a very spiritual event. He had just been baptized, it was amazing and now He was going to get alone with His Father in the desert. You might think that this would be a time when He would be free from temptation. Sometimes we let our guard down when we are leaving an event or a retreat when we just got really close to the Lord. Beware! 1 Corinthians 10:12 says, "So, if you think you are standing firm, be careful that you don't fall!" Let me be really honest with you here. Some of the times when I have been most under attack are when I am in the car on the way home or just getting back from a very spiritual event. I have been tempted on the way home from teaching Disciple Now where I saw amazing works of God and after returning from taking high schoolers to camp. By tempted, I mean, I may have been with a guy that was there with me and we are feeling close because of the experience we just shared and caught myself wanting to be physical with him when I knew I shouldn't.

The other time we are most often tempted is when we are worn down. Christ had been fasting for 40 days when Satan told Him to turn the stones to bread. That would've sounded pretty good to me! In sexual temptation, you've been making out with a guy, you're both resisting going any further, and then… you just give in. You're exhausted from trying to fight off the temptation and after a while, it started to look pretty good to you. You were probably even able to justify it in your mind at the time. Be aware of this, Satan is working. He is looking for that "opportune time" just as he did with Jesus.

I want you to be aware of the Enemy and his schemes, but more importantly, I want us to learn from Christ's example how we should respond in these situations. Did you notice how Christ responded to each temptation? Look back over the story, I said it three times. How did He respond?

Christ _____ with _____.

Jesus knew God's Word so well that He knew how to respond with Truth in every tempting situation. Following Christ's example, we are going to practice facing a tempting lie with truth from the Word.

Please read the lies in the first column and then read the scriptures in the second column. Draw lines connecting the truth that directly combats the lie:

LIE	TRUTH
God is withholding good from you	Forgetting what is behind and straining toward what is ahead, I press on toward the goal to win the prize for which God has called me heavenward in Christ Jesus. (Phil 3:14)
It's not a big deal if you have sex before marriage	Do you not know that your body is a temple of the Holy Spirit...You are not your own; you were bought at a price. Therefore honor God with your body. (1 Cor 6:18-20)
Christians make too much out of premarital sex, God doesn't really care what I do with my body	And God is faithful; he will not let you be tempted beyond what you can bear. But when you are tempted, he will also provide a way out so that you can stand up under it. (1 Cor 10:13b)
You should just give in, you'll never be able to resist the temptation	And we know that in all things God works for the good of those who love him, who have been called according to his purpose. (Romans 8:28)
You've already messed up, you should just keep doing it	Be self-controlled and alert. Your enemy the devil prowls around like a roaring lion looking for someone to devour. (1 Pet 5:8)
Satan isn't scheming to hurt you, he has bigger fish to fry	...there is now no condemnation for those who are in Christ Jesus,... (Romans 8:1)
God will never forgive you for what you've already done	Marriage should be honored by all, and the marriage bed kept pure, for God will judge the adulterer and all the sexually immoral. (Hebrews 13:4)

Christ was equipped to fight off Satan's attacks. He had God's Word ready to combat each lie. I challenge you to do the same—to fight off attacks by putting God's Word in your heart and mind. Be ready with God's Word BEFORE you get into tempting situations and remember to "Watch and pray so that you will not fall into temptation. The spirit is willing, but the body is weak"(Mark 14:38).

Why does God want you to wait to have sex until you are married? Is it true that He is just trying to withhold something amazing from you to play tricks on you? Don't believe that lie from the Enemy. Remember, John 10:10 says, "The thief comes only to steal and kill and destroy; I have come that they may have life, and have it to the full. "Satan is the thief. He wants to take away your purity and destroy you with the often devastating consequences of pre-marital sex. If you think I'm being dramatic, let me just list a few of the possible consequences:

_____HIV

_____STDs

_____Getting pregnant

_____Becoming a teen parent

_____Not being able to give that "gift" to your husband

_____Emotional devastation

_____Marital struggle

Look at the list again and rank them in order of the three consequences that scare you the most. (Put a 1 next to the scariest consequence, a 2 by the next, and a 3 by the third scariest consequence.) One outcome that is a very real possibility is that you could contract a disease or an STD.

From *Don't Date Naked*, p. 76:

> If HIV weren't enough, we have a rat's nest of other sexually transmitted diseases to worry about. One in four—that's twenty five percent for those of you keeping score at home—teens having sex will acquire an STD. More than twenty STDs have been identified, according to the National Institutes of Health, and it's an impressive roll call: chlamydia, herpes, genital warts, gonorrhea, and syphilis comprise the STD all-stars.
>
> These STDS are incredibly easy to pick up if you're sleeping around with someone who's been sleeping around. Dr. C. Everett Koop, the former U.S. Surgeon General, once warned, "When you have sex with someone, you are having sex with everyone they have had sex with for the last ten years, and everyone their partners have had sex with for the last ten years.

When I read this, I had to pick my jaw up off the ground. one in four, ladies, one in four. I hope that is rocking your boat a little bit to realize that if you are standing in a room with eight of your friends that have had sex, two of them have an STD. You are not free from this statistic. If you have sex before marriage, you are included in this group. Don't think to yourself, "Oh, that would never happen to me," or "Well, I would use protection." Neither of those statements is true and condoms or birth control can't guarantee protection. What about the Surgeon General's quote? It better have grossed you out! Let it sink in and never forget it. When you have sex with someone, you are having sex with everyone they've slept with.

Save it. Treasure it. Safeguard your purity so that when the time comes, you can give the gift of your whole self to your husband. You will save yourself from so much hurt and pain if you will commit yourself to purity. What Satan desired to harm you with, the Lord desires to use for your good. Remember our scripture from John 10 that said the thief comes to steal, kill and destroy. Don't neglect to remember the second part of the verse, the hallelujah part, "I have come that they may have life, and have it to the full."

I want you to think about your purity wrapped up as a beautiful gift. The paper is exquisite, every crease perfect, no tape showing and the bow…oh the bow! It is beyond magnificent with its ribbons flowing down the sides of the gift. But what's inside this beautiful package is even more wonderful because it holds your purity—your physical and emotional purity. When we take a look at the gift tag on the box, to whom do you think it is addressed?

Let me read you what it says…the instructions are very specific:
TO: Jesus, who will keep this safe in His care until my wedding day.

Miraculously, on your wedding day, the previous address is erased and in the most beautiful red ink now reads…
TO: The man who has guarded the purity of My princess, her husband. Enjoy!

What you have to decide is what you are going to have in that box for your husband to open. You get to choose how much of yourself you are going to save just for him. Will you save the kisses for only him? Will you save "I love you" for only him? Will you save where you've been touched for only him? Will you save intercourse for only him?

The choice is yours. You decide what you want to save up for your future mate. How can you give God the most glory in your purity? This is not for me to decide. It must be something that you get on your face before the Lord about and ask for conviction from His Spirit. Please don't set up rules for yourself just for rules sake, because "...they lack any value in restraining sensual indulgence" (Colossians 2:23). Instead, let it be a matter of the heart, a decision to glorify God in dating by remaining pure.

Once you have talked to the Lord about what you want to keep in your gift to your husband, we have to address how we keep those things in there. Remember how we talked about temptation? We established that one of the ways we fight temptation is by storing away scripture in our hearts so that we take any deceptive thoughts captive (2 Corinthians 10:5) and replace it with the truth of God's Word. Another way we flee temptation is by setting purity boundaries.

Think of boundaries like road signs. As you travel along the dating highway, these boundaries will be there to help keep you on track and out of danger. For example, let's say that you have a dating boundary that you will not be alone with a guy. You've set this boundary in order to guard your conviction to prevent groping and serious making out. So, when the roommates leave and you are alone with your date, warning signs appear:

STOP. DANGER AHEAD. USE CAUTION. DETOUR. ROAD AHEAD UNSAFE.

Have you set boundaries to protect your gift? The boundaries or "purity protectors" are going to help us make good decisions in "...moments when we must choose between what our bodies crave and what we know our Lord has instructed" (Boy Meets Girl, Joshua Harris, p. 144). We have to set these boundaries ahead of time, because in the heat of the moment you won't be thinking clearly and your convictions will be cloudy.

Once again, let me make it clear that I am not going to tell you what your boundaries should be. I will not give you rules to break. What I will do is offer you suggestions of boundaries that have worked for me or others I know. Then, it is up to you and the Lord to set your boundaries based on how you will best show His glory through your purity. I believe so strongly that the greater boundary you set, the more you will be saved from pain and heartache.

I must share a boundary with you that came to me by way of a song. Here's how it happened: I ran into a sweet friend on the treadmill and we chatted about how this study was coming along and I told her that I was all about dudes and dating right now. I had been reading new books and the old ones I read while still in the dating game. I told her that I was specifically writing about purity and when I did, her eyes lit up and she said, "Oh, Kate, do I have something to share with you. You are gonna love this!" She told me that in her health class, when they came to the topic of abstinence, she brought in a speaker to teach the class. My friend's favorite part of the lesson was this little song she taught the students to help them set boundaries. You may have heard it, it goes a little something like this: "STOP! Don't touch me there. This is my NO NO square!"

How great is that? I have to tell you that I was so tickled by her little ditty that I almost walked right off of that treadmill and straight home to share it with you. The motions are key; here's what you do. When you say, "STOP", put out your hand like you're telling someone to stop. Then, wag your finger back and forth as you say, "Don't touch me there." Then take your hands and make a square, like you're voque-ing, around your torso, from your neck to your upper thigh and say, "This is my no, no square." I thought that was such a cute example of how to say, "This area is off limits!" Here are some other purity protectors you might consider. Unfortunately, none of these come with a song:

- Nothing from the neck down
- Saving "I love you" until there is an engagement ring on your finger
- "Open door policy;" no time alone together in a room with the door closed
- Visiting boys leave before dark
- No alone time together on couch with movie

These are all examples of boundaries that will help protect the gift you want to give only to your husband. Please remember that these are only outward acts of what is truly a heart issue. The decision must come first from a desire to serve God by abstaining from sexual intimacy. If your heart is not in the right place, you will break your boundaries and probably forget why you even made them in the first place.

The path to purity is a hard one to travel alone. Friends, accountability partners and possibly parents are great resources to help keep you on track. As you get serious about your purity, consider having an accountability partner who is not afraid to ask you the tough questions about what you've been doing with your boyfriend. Be sure that you are communicating with the guy you're dating about your convictions. If he doesn't have the same commitment to purity as you do, realize that this is not the type of guy you need to date.

You may have been reading this chapter thinking, "I have messed up so bad in the past. I have already given so much of myself away. I feel like I have practically nothing left to give only my husband." If feelings of shame and guilt are getting in the way of you pursuing purity, let me tell you that our God is a Great Healer and a Mighty Redeemer. The blood He shed for us on the cross washes us so that though are sins are as scarlet, He has washed us white as snow (1saiah 1:18). No matter what you have done, you must believe that there is "...now no condemnation for those who are in Christ Jesus" (Romans 8:1). The Mighty Redeemer desires to restore all of you and the Great Healer wants to take away the pain of the past. Dear sister, please allow God's forgiveness to wash over you and set you free. David, a man who knew God's forgiveness for his own sexual impurity, prayed this in the 103rd Psalm:

> Praise the LORD, O my soul; all my inmost being, praise his holy name.
>
> Praise the LORD, O my soul, and forget not all his benefits-
>
> who forgives all your sins and heals all your diseases
>
> who redeems your life from the pit and crowns you with love and compassion,
>
> who satisfies your desires with good things so that your youth is renewed like the eagle's...
>
> The LORD is compassionate and gracious, slow to anger, abounding in love...
>
> he does not treat us as our sins deserve or repay us according to our iniquities.
>
> For as high as the heavens are above the earth, so great is his love for those who fear him;
>
> as far as the east is from the west, so far has he removed our transgressions from us.
>
> As a father has compassion on his children, so the LORD has compassion on those who fear him;
>
> for he knows how we are formed, he remembers that we are dust.
>
> As for man, his days are like grass, he flourishes like a flower of the field;
>
> the wind blows over it and it is gone, and its place remembers it no more.

Many times have I prayed this psalm and thanked God for removing my sins and having compassion on me. I have had to return to my knees and cry out for forgiveness and every time, I've received cleansing and renewal. Don't let your past be your present. God is a God of new mercies and forgiveness TODAY. Let Him remove all of the guilt and shame and offer your purity to you once again, white as snow.

Our amazing God is deeply in love with each of us. He desires to know us intimately, lead us as we date and guard our purity. Let His love be all that you need. Allow Him to hold you close and make you complete. Let His blood wash over you and make you clean.

Before we turn the page and begin our next topic, please take a moment and allow this song to be your prayer to your Captivating Creator.

> Your face is beautiful
> And Your eyes are like the stars
> Your gentle hands have healing
> There inside the scars
> Your loving arms they draw me near
> And Your smile it brings me peace
> Draw me closer oh my Lord
> Draw me closer Lord to Thee
> Captivate us Lord Jesus set our eyes on You
> Devastate us with your presence falling down
> And rushing river draw us nearer
> Holy fountain consume us with You
> Captivate us Lord Jesus with You

Captivate Us – Watermark

Can you remember the three must-packs we added to our list of 15 in this chapter? Try to fill in the blanks from memory. If you need to, take a look back in the chapter for the answers.

8TH MUST-PACK:_____

9TH MUST-PACK:_____

10TH MUST-PACK:_____

Good job! All of the work we've done in the past three chapters is laying the foundation for a God glorifying college experience. We did a lot of digging and a lot of work on ourselves in Dudes and Dating. I hope that you've got your heart resting safe in the Lord's hands and that you are ready to give Him your whole body, His temple.

YOUR
TEMPLE

Think for a moment about what our culture has to say about beauty. Let images of the "ideal" woman" parade through your mind. Stand in the checkout line at the grocery store amidst the mass of magazines and think about the models on the covers. Let your mind scroll through TV spots and commercials for skin care lines, weight loss pills, gym equipment and fashion accessories. What images are coming to your mind? Through this media onslaught and what you've viewed in our culture, what does the world profess to be the "ideal" or "most beautiful"?

List here what the world says are the "must-haves" to beauty:

Are you feeling as exhausted as I am after completing my list? I'm tired from just thinking about all I would have to do to live up to the world's standards. I guess the first step would be to make sure I wash my face at night and put on moisturizer instead of just crawling into bed!

Here are some of the "must-haves" from my list: clear, flawless skin; thin bodies; muscular, fit bodies; straight, white teeth; tan skin; big, long eyelashes; manicured nails and toes; silky, flowing hair; fashion-forward attire.

Can't you just see the commercial or magazine cover in your mind promoting each of these attributes? Everywhere we turn someone is telling us what to buy to make us look better and more like the "ideal." To me, the whole idea of the "ideal" is comical. Who are these people that sit up in their lofty skyscrapers in places like LA and NYC or on couches on the E! Network that get to decide what everyone should want to look like? Who are they to decide? Why should we listen to them anyway? Surely you know by now that in a moments notice "they" will change their minds on what is "in". Whether it's the latest fashion trend that changes from the slacker look of the early 90s to the current boho-chic (which, ironically, won't be in style once you're reading this!) or the long, sleek locks turned short and sassy; it will always change.

These "people," the overpaid and over-idolized editors and models, are not the ones from which we should take our cues. I want you to see that **the world's definition of beauty is fickle and has changed continually over the centuries.** This article, "Body Image, Media and Eating Disorders" from the Academic Psychiatry Journal provided a great history lesson:

Throughout history, the standard of female beauty often has been unrealistic and difficult to attain. Those with money and higher socioeconomic status were far more likely to be able to conform to these standards. Women typically were willing to sacrifice comfort and even endure pain to achieve them.

In colonial times, the harsh environment and lack of comfortable surroundings required that all family members contribute to survival. Large families were preferred as children could help tend to the land and household chores. For these reasons, communities valued fertile, physically strong and able women.

However, in the 19th century, ideals shifted and women with tiny waists and large bustles came to be valued. It was desirable for an upper-class man to be able to span a woman's waist with his hands. If women were too frail to work, plantation owners could justify the use of slaves. Indeed, much emphasis was placed on female fragility, which then made a woman a more attractive candidate for marriage. The ideal wealthy woman of the time was sickly and prone to headaches; the fine art of fainting was taught in finishing schools throughout the country. Women of significant financial means would go as far as having ribs removed to further decrease their waist size. Despite being painful and causing health problems, such as shortness of breath (which could lead to pneumonia) and dislocated visceral organs, corsets became the height of fashion.

Some have said that the invention of the corset was the main impetus for the feminist movement at the beginning of the 20th century. Women turned up their noses at complicated dresses, instead favoring pants, which were comfortable and did not restrict movement. They cut their hair short, bound their breasts, took up cigarette smoking, and fought for the right to vote. At this point, it was fashionable to be angular, thin, and boyish-looking, and manufacturers routinely featured pictures of "flappers" in their advertisements.

During the Second World War, ideals changed yet again. With their husbands overseas, young women went to work so that industry could thrive. In their spare time, some of them formed professional sports teams. Again, society valued competent, strong, and physically able women. However, things changed after the war. The men came home and cultural values shifted again to emphasize traditional family and gender roles. Women took to wearing dresses and skirts. Again highlighting the importance of fertility (this time period marked the beginning of the Baby Boom era), the population favored a more curvaceous frame like that of Marilyn Monroe.

In the 1960s, major changes were in the works...Similar to the trends found during the suffrage movement at the beginning of the century, women of the decade idealized thin and boyish bodies like that of the emaciated supermodel Twiggy.

The current media culture is complicated and very confusing. Women are told that they can and should "have it all." They expect family, career, and home to be perfect, and Martha Stewart tells them how to do it. The media inundates them with mixed messages about what is sexy, making it difficult to choose a role model. The heroin chic waif made popular by Kate Moss in the early 1990s competes with the voluptuous Baywatch babe personified by Pamela Anderson and the athletic soccer stars who celebrated a World Cup victory by tearing their shirts off. Though it is highly unlikely for a rail-thin woman to have natural DD-cup size breasts, toy manufacturers set this expectation by developing and marketing the Barbie doll, whose measurements are physiologically impossible."

(Academic Psychiatry, 30:3, May-June 2006 http://ap.psychiatryonline.org, p. 258)

Fill in the timeline below by drawing or writing the description of the "ideal" body type and/or fashion during the specific time period:

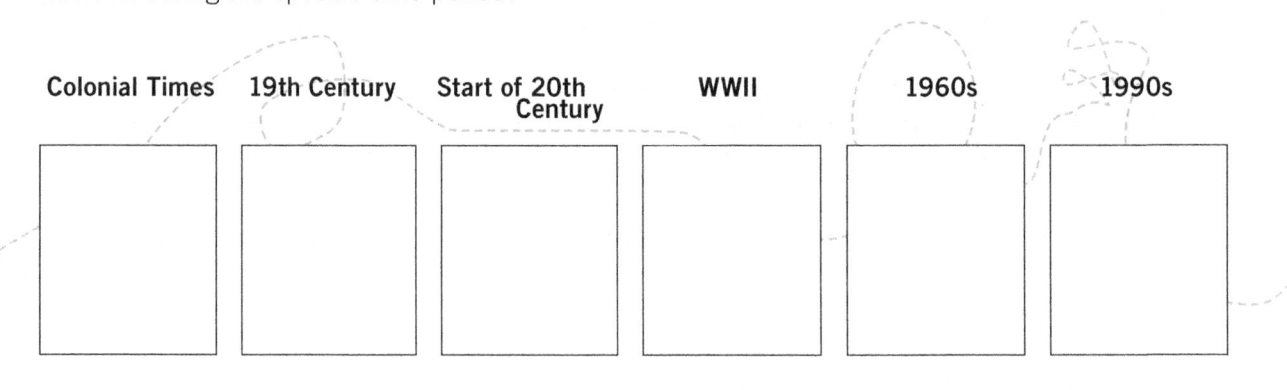

Colonial Times	19th Century	Start of 20th Century	WWII	1960s	1990s

I have to chuckle when I look back over the absurdity of history! Removing ribs, wearing corsets that caused organs to dislocate, binding breasts, plastic surgery to look like Barbie! What were we thinking? Or what are we thinking… as Joel Yager, M.D. so poignantly notes: "Every society has a way of torturing its women, whether by binding their feet or by sticking them into whalebone corsets. What contemporary American culture has come up with is designer jeans" (Academic Psychiatry, 30:3, May-June 2006 http://ap.psychiatryonline.org, p.257). Oh, how I have tortured myself to get into a pair of jeans! I know this quote to be true for me and I also know that the torture doesn't stop there.

Before we move on, I want to make sure that you got the point. What is the first reason I gave you for why we shouldn't get our beauty cues from the folks in the Hollywood?

1. The world's definition of beauty has continually _____ over the centuries.

The women of the past have had their share of pain in their attempts to conform to the world's "ideal" but today's woman's struggle is intensified by the bombardment of a powerful media presence. Just like we talked about at the beginning of this chapter, there are media messages everywhere we turn that seek to influence our thinking. I was shocked about the reality of the media's power when I read the information from this study:

> No discussion of body image and the media would be complete without referencing Becker's landmark study comparing rates of eating disorders before and after the arrival of television in Fiji in 1995. Ethnic Fijians have traditionally encouraged healthy appetites and have preferred a more rotund body type, which signified wealth and the ability to care for one's family. Strong cultural identity is thought to be protective against eating disorders; there was only one case of anorexia nervosa reported on the island prior to 1995. However, in 1998, rates of dieting skyrocketed from 0 to 69%, and young people routinely cited the appearance of the attractive actors on shows like "Beverly Hills 90210" and "Melrose Place" as the inspiration for their weight loss. For the first time, inhabitants of the island began to exhibit disordered eating. (Academic Psychiatry, 30:3, May-June 2006 http://ap.psychiatryonline.org, p. 258-259)

Don't be fooled into thinking that there is not a war going on for your mind every day. Don't be misled into believing that these people are trying to help you out by making you look better. Realize that **they are not interested in your well-being but the almighty dollar.** This powerful, money-making industry is called the Beauty Industry. Can you put a price tag on beauty? Evidently so, because the beauty industry reports an estimated $29 billion dollars worth of business each year (Beth Moore, Esther, p. 37 quoted Mary Lisa Gavenas Color Stories (New York: Simon & Schuster, 2002), 10.

The second reason we shouldn't get our beauty cues from the "beauty industry"?

2.   Their concern is not your well-being. It is for the _____.

Another major problem with the beauty industry is their promotion of false ideals. Did you know that "twenty-five years ago, the average fashion model was 8% thinner than the average woman? Today, that number has risen to 23%" (Academic Psychiatry, 30:3, May-June 2006 http://ap.psychiatryonline.org, p. 258-259). The models on the runways represent a small percentage of women who were either "lucky" enough to be born into the current ultimate body or are willing to torture themselves to look that way.

The Dove Campaign for Real Beauty was launched in 2004 "to serve as a starting point for societal change and act as a catalyst for widening the definition and discussion of beauty" (http://www.dove.us/#/CFRB/arti_cfrb.aspx[cp-documentid=7049726]/, Campaign for Real Beauty Mission, 3/14/08). Maybe you've seen some of their commercials or magazine ads. I remember the ear to ear smile that came across my face the first time I saw a "real beauty" commercial. I was so proud of the attempts they were making to take a stand against the **unrealistic and unattainable beauty expectations.** "Evolution" is a powerful video that Dove hosts on their website. The one-minute video starts with a woman who looks like I do when I first roll out of bed and shows how through hair and make-up, lighting, airbrushing and re-touching this woman is transformed into a super-model that is print-ad ready. It is a startling look at the amount of work that goes into creating the "ideal" and an amusing glimpse into the ridiculousness of the same. We have been lied to, tricked and told to achieve an ideal that is truly unachievable.

The third reason we shouldn't get our cues from the "beauty industry"?

3. They promote _____ and _____ beauty expectations.

Some celebrities and a rare few in the industry like Dove are beginning to take notice of the detrimental effects this is having on our young women. One such celebrity was Jamie Lee Curtis. You might remember her from *Freaky Friday*.

In 2002, actress Jamie Lee Curtis famously posed for *More* magazine, both in typical "glammed up" attire and then in her sports bra and shorts. The reality is that most magazines airbrush photos and use expensive computer technology to correct blemishes and hide figure flaws. In fact, in Jamie Lee's own words, she has "very big breasts and a soft, fatty little tummy... and... back fat." She felt that women should know that the figures portrayed by the media are rarely real. Granted, celebrities can afford to hire personal trainers and nutritionists to assist in their weight loss endeavors. Stylists select fetching outfits and tailors wait on standby to make sure that clothes fit like second skin. Before awards ceremonies, attendees routinely fast and endure tight-fitting undergarments to flatten their stomachs for unforgiving evening gowns. (Academic Psychiatry, 30:3, May-June 2006 http://ap.psychiatryonline.org, p. 258)

The beauty industry and their marketing machine has so destroyed the self image of women that very few women see themselves as beautiful and many hate their bodies so much that they are damaging them through eating disorders, addiction to exercise and cutting.

Dove's website provides several startling statistics that they found from their global study, "The Real Truth about Beauty: A Global Report."

What percentage would you guess their findings showed of women around the world who would describe themselves as beautiful? (circle one)

2%   5%   7%   13%

The answer: two percent. If the Dove study is true, the majority of us have looked in the mirror and been unsatisfied with what we see. We compare our reflection to the magazine cover. We are dissatisfied with how we were made. I know this struggle personally. I worked tirelessly to make my body into what I believed it was supposed to look like. I was exhausted and sick.

Are you part of the 98%? Do you see yourself as flawed? Do you look in the mirror and hate what you see? Are you doing things to yourself that may damage your body in order to attain the world's "ideal"? Are you hurting, sad, depressed and frustrated? My heart goes out to you because there was a time when I lived in that 98%. I lived in the constant nightmare of my self-loathing. I found a reflection everywhere I turned and used it as an opportunity to further criticize my imperfection.

I worked at a Young Life camp in Colorado during the summer after my freshman year while still struggling with my desire for physical perfection. I went out on a run one morning. I remember crying out to the Lord as my feet pounded the ground, telling Him how dissatisfied I was with myself. I remember stopping suddenly and becoming very aware of my surroundings. Before me, I saw a field of beautiful wildflowers in a brilliant assortment of color. Behind them stood tall mountains topped with snow and the backdrop was a clear blue sky. My breath caught in my chest as I realized at once what the Lord was helping me to see.

I would never tell Him that He had incorrectly colored a flower or that the placement of a mountain peak was off. What audacity! How dare I! Yet, I too was the work of His hand and I questioned the way He created me. Romans 9:20 mirrored my thoughts, "But who are you, O man, to talk back to God?" Shall what is formed say to him who formed it, 'Why did you make me like this?'"

I dropped to my knees, thanked God for creating me perfectly, with even more care than any of this and submitted my thoughts to Him completely. I asked Him to free me and to help me see myself rightly. I returned to my room after that jog and penned this little poem:

> Lord,
> I am so amazed by Your creation
> The way the sun highlights the mountains
> The way the sky lies so beautifully behind them
> The trees are a reminder of Your majesty
> The flowers that adorn the ground remind me of Your sweet mercies
> You have made each piece so perfectly
> You are the Great Artist
> I am humbled to know that You are the same Creator who formed me
> As perfectly as You created every tree and every blade of grass,
> You have created me.
> Hallelujah

Was my journey easy after that? No. I had good days and bad but I consistently knew where I found my worth. I was forever changed from being a self-loather to realizing that I was a masterpiece of the Great Artist. The tears fill my eyes as I remember the pain of that life and thankfulness floods my soul as I praise my Redeemer for freeing me from that existence of bondage to my thoughts.

I want you to know that we serve a Mighty God who comes equipped with holy bolt cutters. He desires to come and break away each of those chains that are binding you. He wants to give you freedom to walk in the newness of life and to be set free to dance again (Psalm 30:11).

If you are struggling with an eating disorder or any form of self hatred, please know that our Gracious Lord offers us freedom. 2 Corinthians 3:17 says, "Now the Lord is the Spirit, and where the Spirit of the Lord is, there is freedom." A major part of my journey to freedom was becoming aware of all the lies about my worth that I believed. I believed it when the culture told me I wasn't good enough or pretty enough. However, I have learned that I don't get cues about my self-image and value from them. Do you remember the three main reasons why we don't? Look back through the lesson and write them in here.

1. _____

2. _____

3. _____

The final and ultimate reason we don't listen to the beauty industry is that **they didn't create us!** As I realized that day in the mountains, I am a creation of the Ultimate Sculptor and the Divine Designer. I look to Him to find my worth.

I want you to be aware of what the beauty industry is teaching you, but we do not stop at what the world has to say about beauty. **We are aware but we don't stay there!** We are aware of Satan's schemes to destroy us but we will not allow him the pleasure. With my fist in the air I have proclaimed Micah 7:8, "Do not gloat over me, my enemy! Though I have fallen, I will rise. Though I sit in darkness, the LORD will be my light."

Let's rise. Let's take a stand against this false concept of beauty and turn our eyes to Jesus and learn from Him. We must take all of these lies that seek to destroy us and take them captive. Then, we replace our thoughts with the thoughts of our gracious Lord. Remember, ladies, this world is not our home. We do not get our cues from our culture. We are aliens and strangers here. We follow the One who made us and loves us, desires our good and could care less about the bottom line.

Therefore we must pack the next item into our suitcase:

11TH MUST-PACK:
DO NOT CONFORM; BE TRANSFORMED

This must-pack is based on Romans 12:2:

> Do not conform any longer to the pattern of this world, but be transformed by the renewing of your mind. Then you will be able to test and approve what God's will is—his good, pleasing and perfect will.

The Bible Knowledge Commentary explains our transformation like this:

> The Greek verb translated "transformed" (*metamorphousthe*) is seen in the English word "metamorphosis," a total change from inside out. The key to this change is the "mind" (*noos*), the control center of one's attitudes, thoughts, feelings, and actions. As one's mind keeps on being made new by the spiritual input of God's Word, prayer, and Christian fellowship, his lifestyle keeps on being transformed.

"Metamorphosis" reminds me of my grade school lesson on butterflies. I remember watching a slide show about the lifecycle of the butterfly. It began as a caterpillar that formed a cocoon, and then miraculously emerged as a beautiful butterfly. Have you been like the caterpillar—inching through this life, scraping your body against the destructive dirt of this world as you try to make it through each day? God is calling you to a transformation, a metamorphosis. Let's wrap ourselves in the cocoon of His Word and learn what He has to say to us so that we can emerge as beautiful butterflies, set free to soar above the cares of the world.

Take a moment in the embrace of God's holy Word. I would like to first offer you the world's thoughts that persuade us to conform to our culture and then provide you with the transforming truths from scripture.

The world may tell you that "appearance is everything" but our transforming thoughts from scripture tell us:

> But the LORD said to Samuel, "Do not consider his appearance or his height, for I have rejected him. The LORD does not look at the things man looks at. Man looks at the outward appearance, but the LORD looks at the heart." (1 Samuel 16:7)

> Charm is deceptive, and beauty is fleeting; but a woman who fears the LORD is to be praised. (Proverbs 31:30)

Though the world focuses on fashion, scripture transforms those ideas:

> Your beauty should not come from outward adornment, such as braided hair and the wearing of gold jewelry and fine clothes. Instead, it should be that of your inner self, the unfading beauty of a gentle and quiet spirit, which is of great worth in God's sight. For this is the way the holy women of the past who put their hope in God used to make themselves beautiful. (1 Peter 3:3-5a)

The models on the magazines teach us how to offer our bodies as tools for advertisement, lust and envy. God's Word tells us:

> Therefore, I urge you, brothers, in view of God's mercy, to offer your bodies as living sacrifices, holy and pleasing to God—this is your spiritual act of worship. (Romans 12:1)

Are you beginning to feel your wings? The freedom of the Word excites me into taking flight. Stay in that cocoon for just a minute—we're about ready to fly.

The world may tell you that you are "messed up", damaged and full of imperfections but God's powerful, transforming Word has this to say:

> Yet, O LORD, you are our Father. We are the clay, you are the potter; we are all the work of your hand. (Isaiah 64:8)

David was able to see Himself as God's creation and praised the Lord for His handiwork:

> For you created my inmost being; you knit me together in my mother's womb. I praise you because I am fearfully and wonderfully made; your works are wonderful, I know that full well. My frame was not hidden from you when I was made in the secret place. When I was woven together in the depths of the earth, your eyes saw my unformed body. All the days ordained for me were written in your book before one of them came to be. (Psalm 139:13-16)

Allow the Lord to relay these truths to you. If you'd allow me the liberty, I'm going to switch the verse up and put God in the first person. He says to you:

> I created your inmost being; I knit you together in your mother's womb. Praise me because I made you fearfully and wonderfully; my works are wonderful, you know that. Your frame was not hidden from me when I made you in the secret place. You were woven together in the depths of the earth, I saw your unformed body. All the days ordained for you were written in my book before one of them came to be.

Dear sister, *you are beautiful*; not because of the world's opinion but because you are a creation of the Sovereign Lord God! Think about His creation, His works are wonderful!

Through my study of Psalm 139, I was able to see the theme of knitting or weaving. "You knit me together" and "when I was woven together" paint a picture of an artist intimately concerned with his work. Several commentaries referred to "the unformed body" as the embryo. In light of our knitting theme, it is as though our Creator took this mass and wove it into the most beautiful tapestry. Adam Clarke's Commentary described God in this context as the Divine Artificer. I wanted to look around the room after reading it to see if I was the only one who had no idea what "artificer" meant. But it was okay! I'm all alone here in my little home office and nobody has to know that I have to go to the dictionary to find out what it means. Here's what I found: Merriam-Webster.com defines artificer as "a skilled or artistic worker or craftsman."

That means that our God is the Divinely Skilled and Wonderfully Artistic Craftsman. He is the Great Artist and you are His masterpiece. You are the pinnacle of creation. After He had created everything, He created man and woman.

You may have been convinced that all of your make-up and your perfectly styled hair is what made you most attractive to others. 2 Corinthians 3:12-18 provides our most attractive quality:

> Therefore, since we have such a hope, we are very bold. We are not like Moses, who would put a veil over his face to keep the Israelites from gazing at it while the radiance was fading away... Now the Lord is the Spirit, and where the Spirit of the Lord is, there is freedom. And we, who with unveiled faces all reflect the Lord's glory, are being transformed into his likeness with ever-increasing glory, which comes from the Lord, who is the Spirit.

Did you see it in there? As living vessels for God's Holy Spirit, we display from our faces what Moses had to veil. When Moses came down from seeing God pass by on the mountain, the glory of God shone so brightly from his face that he had to veil himself. However, we are told that with unveiled faces we reflect the Lord's glory. Our radiance comes from the Lord. Have you ever met someone whose love relationship with the Lord was just written all over his/her face? There is a gentleness, tenderness and kindness that radiates from a devout Christ follower. You leave being with that person feeling encouraged and uplifted. That is the kind of beauty I want to seek after, the beauty that comes from getting close to the Lord. I desire that my most attractive quality would be His glory emanating from me.

I love what Isaiah 61:3b has to say:

They will be called oaks of righteousness, a planting of the LORD for the display of his splendor.

Ladies, our self image issues fade when we realize that it is not about us. The purpose of this body is not to display how attractive we are but to show how amazing God is. I hope that is a freeing thought for you. I hope it helps you lift from the drudgery of trying to crawl through the world, conforming to their standards and transforms you into a woman set free to soar above the world's definition of beauty. Be transformed! **Focus your efforts not on your mirror reflection but on your Christ reflection!**

The purpose of our bodies is to display all that He is. He calls our earthly bodies His temple. Check out these scriptures. As you read them, circle the word **"temple"** each time you see it:

Don't you know that you yourselves are God's temple and that God's Spirit lives in you? If anyone destroys God's temple, God will destroy him; for God's temple is sacred, and you are that temple (1 Corinthians 3:16-17).

Do you not know that your body is a temple of the Holy Spirit, who is in you, whom you have received from God? You are not your own; you were bought at a price. Therefore honor God with your body (1 Corinthians 6:19-20).

… for we are the temple of the living God... (2 Corinthians 6:16)

I did not see a temple in the city, because the Lord God Almighty and the Lamb are its temple (Revelation 21:22).

I want us to get some deeper understanding to what it means that our body is God's temple. If you've always thought of the "temple" in the context of the Old Testament, that's okay because we are going to start there. The temple actually started as a tabernacle or a tent. The Lord desired to have a mobile dwelling place for His glory as the Israelites traveled through the desert.

We first learn about the tabernacle in the 25th chapter of Exodus while Moses was with God on Mount Sinai. While Moses was up there those 40 days and nights, God commanded Moses to make a tabernacle for Him. In Exodus 25:8, God told Moses, "Then have them make a sanctuary for me, and I will dwell among them. Make this tabernacle and all its furnishings exactly like the pattern I will show you." The details of the tabernacle construction, its furnishings, and priests and their duties take up six chapters! The Lord, and rightly so, has the most specific taste in how He wanted His dwelling place decorated. Let me give you an idea of how specific He was. Here's a little sample of the extent of the detail taken from Exodus 26:1-6 as He explains how He wants the tabernacle, or tent, to be made:

Make the tabernacle with ten curtains of finely twisted linen and blue, purple and scarlet yarn, with cherubim worked into them by a skilled craftsman. All the curtains are to be the same size—twenty-eight cubits long and four cubits wide. Join five of the curtains together, and do the same with the other five. Make loops of blue material along the edge of the end curtain in one set, and do the same with the end curtain in the other set. Make fifty loops on one curtain and fifty loops on the end curtain of the other set, with the loops opposite each other. Then make fifty gold clasps and use them to fasten the curtains together so that the tabernacle is a unit.

Can you even imagine if you were an interior decorator and your client came in with something like this! What a tall order to fill! All joking aside, every part of the construction of this tabernacle and everything it contained reflected God's glory. He knew precisely how it should be. Later, when the Israelites settled in Jerusalem, Solomon built a temple to the Lord; a permanent place where the Israelites would come and worship Him. The construction of the temple is found in 1 Kings where King Solomon used great care to construct a temple for the Lord that followed the pattern of the tabernacle. After it was constructed and the Ark of the Covenant, a symbolic representation of God's presence, was brought into the temple, God's glory filled the place (1 Kings 8:11). The temple was regarded as the holy place of God's indwelling. The priests took great care of the temple and those that desecrated it were punished.

Now, let's jump in our time travel machine and span the time between the OT (Old Testament) and the NT (New Testament). Do you remember what our scriptures above told us? Look back, specifically at 2 Corinthians 6:16 and fill in the blank:

For _____ are the _____ of the living God...

You, my sister in Christ, are a temple of the living God!

> In the Old Testament God's glory was in the temple, which represented His presence with the people. In this Age God dwells in His new temple which is constructed not from inanimate materials but of living believers. The Holy Spirit indwells each individual believer, who is thus a "temple" (Bible Knowledge Commentary).

With even more care than that with which He made the temple, He made you. Then, He consecrated you by the blood of Jesus, making you clean, so that His glory could dwell in you. It rocks my world to think that the Almighty God dwells within me. I am a walking, living, breathing indwelling of His holiness.

Such an amazing concept reminds me that I need to take care of this temple He has given me. Do you see the parallel? The Divine Designer spent six chapters explaining to Moses how to build the temple and how to care for it. God was intimately concerned with how His temple would be treated. Now, realize that it would take way more than six chapters to detail how He made you. If you doubt this to be true, take a look at a human anatomy textbook sometime. With greater concern and care than a temple of brick and mortar, He dictated your creation, a temple of flesh and blood. If the Levitical priests devoted themselves to caring and maintaining the temple in Jerusalem, how much more should I care for the temple that is my body.

Let's seek to follow the command to honor God with our bodies, the temple of His holy spirit (1 Corinthians 6:19-20). We follow it by getting out our suitcase and packing in our next must-pack from The Freshman 15. This must-pack is:

12TH 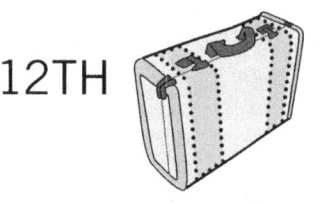 MUST-PACK:
HONOR GOD WITH YOUR BODY (BY WHAT YOU PUT IN IT & ON IT)

What you put in it:

Your college campus is going to spread before you a buffet of substances with an "All You Can Consume" banner flying above. Whether it's the lines and lines of food waiting for you beneath the heat lamps in the dorm cafeteria or the kegs and bottles waiting for you at the parties, they are offered by the plenty!

I want to give you a "heads up" on what you're going to encounter so that you can make God-honoring decisions. Let's start with what will and will not be available to you under the food category. First of all, your mom will no longer be available to cook all of your meals and keep an eye on your nutrition! I grew up with a mother that did all of the grocery shopping, cooked all of the meals, paid attention when we weren't getting enough veggies and made us drink milk—for strong bones, of course.

When I got to college, I had to do the grocery shopping, I had to prepare the meals and I alone had to choose what to eat in restaurants and cafeterias. It was a lot for me to take in, and at times, my diet wasn't overly nutritious. Our cafeteria had a "Make Your Own Waffles" area on the weekends. My friends and I ate enough waffles to sink a ship and I didn't have dear old mom there to warn me against such ignorant behavior. It made me feel horrible and I learned to start tempering some of those sweets with healthier options. I learned to heed the warning from Proverbs 25:16, "If you find honey, eat just enough — too much of it, and you will vomit." I love that little gem of scripture! It's kind of funny but very true.

Scripture provides the bottom line when we approach food. 1 Corinthians 10:31 says, "So whether you eat or drink or whatever you do, do it all for the glory of God." Please don't get bogged down in what you should and shouldn't eat. I want you to keep your heart and mind in correct focus so that when your stomach growls, you know what to do. Seek to glorify God in whatever you eat and drink. We honor God with our bodies by following this command.

Our scripture didn't just talk about glorifying God in what you eat, did it? Nope. Fill in the blank:

Whether you eat or _____ or whatever you do, do it all for the glory of God.

Be mindful of the reason we are here on this earth, why He has given us these earthly vessels, our bodies. We are here to bring glory to God. We want to do that with both the solid substances we take in and the liquid ones. Alcohol, coffee, and energy drinks are available on college campuses by the truckloads. We want to make sure we are honoring God with what we consume. Therefore, I would like to offer you two scriptures to help guide you in your decisions.

The first is one of my favorites that I often use to help me down the path of discernment. It comes from 1 Corinthians 6:12:
"Everything is permissible for me"—but not everything is beneficial.
"Everything is permissible for me"—but I will not be mastered by anything.

Based on this scripture, I would challenge you to ask yourself two questions when confronted with the substances I mentioned.

1. Is it beneficial?
2. Does it or will it have mastery over me?

For example, coffee can be great. Actually, I love coffee. I enjoy the sweet taste and the accompanying eye opening energy boost. I receive nutritional benefits from coffee and a little extra pep in my step. However, this substance does not have mastery over me. I never allow myself to become addicted to coffee and dependent upon the caffeine. We enter the "danger zone" when we allow ourselves to be controlled by anything other than the Holy Spirit.

Here's the second scripture I want you to consider when thinking about substance abuse:

Do not get drunk on wine, which leads to debauchery. Instead, be filled with the Spirit (Ephesians 5:18).

This verse specifically tells us not to get drunk but there is a greater lesson involved. The bigger truth is that we are to be filled with the Spirit. We don't want anything to get in the way of God's power working in us. When we are controlled by the substance, we are not controlled by the Spirit.

Remember that we are God's temple, a holy creation in which the Holy Spirit dwells. We don't want to get in the way of His work within us. "Since we have these promises, dear friends, let us purify ourselves from everything that contaminates body and spirit, perfecting holiness out of reverence for God (2 Corinthians 7:1).

What you put on it:

There was a time when I dressed to draw attention to my body. I wanted to be noticed. My goal was to have every guy in the room look at me and want to talk to me. I was unaware of my sin and of the stumbling block I was putting up for my brothers in Christ. I remember being at church and hearing Jeremy, who was then my youth intern, talking with a group of us and explaining how difficult it was for him to keep his mind pure when girls had their bodies on display everywhere he turned. I had never thought of it like that. I had never imagined that I was leading them to sin. For me, it had been a selfish endeavor in which I was seeking the attention and affection of guys in order to help me feel desired. I realize now that I should have been seeking to allow the Lord to meet those needs.

The Holy Spirit convicted me about my clothes. I no longer wanted to cause anyone to stumble, as Romans 14:13b says, "Instead, make up your mind not to put any stumbling block or obstacle in your brother's way." I named the clothing that I thought revealed too much and might cause impure thoughts, STUMBLE WEAR! With the help of my big sister, we went through my closet and removed all of the articles that might fall into the "stumble wear" category. I committed to displaying the Lord through my modesty and my purity.

Scripture teaches us about modesty in 1 Timothy 2:9 when it says, "I also want women to dress modestly, with decency and propriety, not with braided hair or gold or pearls or expensive clothes, but with good deeds, appropriate for women who profess to worship God." The Bible Knowledge Commentary provided some great application to this scripture:

> Next Paul turned to the females in the congregation. For their adornment they should not emphasize the external, but the internal. They should dress modestly, with decency and propriety. These terms stress not so much the absence of sexual suggestiveness, though it is included, but rather an appearance that is simple, moderate, judicious, and free from ostentation. The specifics Paul mentioned **(braided hair or gold or pearls or expensive clothes) are not wrong in themselves, but become inappropriate when they indicate misplaced values.** In the Ephesian church these styles may have been associated with the local temple prostitutes. Christians must be careful about letting a pagan culture set their fashions. Instead of stressing external beauty, according to the world's standards, **Christian women should manifest a different set of values. They should adorn themselves with good deeds.** They should depend on their faithful service in the name of Christ to render them attractive to others. This was no plea for women to make themselves unattractive; it was simply an exhortation to **reject the world's yardstick for measuring beauty and adopt heaven's standard.** One should expect nothing less from women who profess to worship God (emphasis mine).

Fill in the blanks according to what you just read from the excerpt:

Braided hair, gold, pearls or expensive clothes are not wrong in themselves but become inappropriate

when they _____ _____ _____.

Christian women should adorn themselves with _____ _____ in order to make themselves attractive to others.

We should reject the _____ _____ for measuring beauty and adopt

_____ _____.

I hope we take two lessons away from this scripture. First, remember that your true beauty is due to God's hand in creating you and His radiance through you. Don't get me wrong, I love getting "dolled up" as much as the next gal. However, I am confident that those outer trappings do not change my worth. Whether I'm decked out in the finest clothes, cute accessories and killer heels or I'm hanging out at home in my PJ's, I am confident that I am loved the same. Remember the verse we read in 1 Samuel 16:7 that the world may look at the outward appearance but God is concerned with your heart. 1 Peter 3:3-5a reminded us that the godly women of the past focused on their inner self to make themselves beautiful. As we age, the outer beauty will fade; it is the inner beauty that can continue to grow more beautiful as the years pass.

The second lesson I want us to take away is that our bodies, God's temple, are to be used to glorify Him and not to bring attention to ourselves or cause guys to lust after us. We should desire to cover up instead of stripping down in order to honor God with our bodies.

I found an article about the Christian musician Rebecca St. James on christianitytoday.com that I wanted to share with you. Rebecca has been vocal about her commitment to purity and shared some specifics with how she followed the exhortation toward modesty in her day to day:

> I also try to dress appropriately. I don't show cleavage. I layer thinner T-shirts and wear longer shirts with low-rise jeans. I don't wear skirts that are shorter than where my fingertips rest when I let my arms fall naturally against my body. I think we women need to help our brothers with this whole lust battle because they're getting attacked on every side, and we don't need to contribute to that (Christianity Today International/Today's Christian Woman magazine. March/April 2005, Vol. 27, No. 2, Page 30 http://www.christianitytoday.com/tcw/2005/marapr/1.30.html).

Now that we've packed two more items into our college-bound suitcase, we are almost ready to turn the page to learn about our last three must-packs. Before we move on, please take a moment of reflection by answering a few questions.

1. How do we transform our thoughts?

2. What was the most transforming thought or scripture you read?

3. When we think about what we put in our bodies, we want to remember 1 Corinthians 10:31. Write the verse here:

4. When we think about what we put on our bodies, we want to remember to dress in what way?

5. What does it mean to you that your body is God's temple? How will that affect the way you care for it?

6. What must-packs did we add to our suitcase in this chapter?

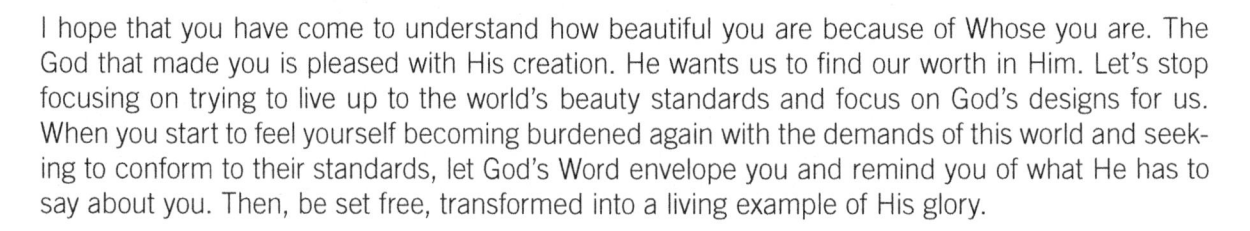

11TH MUST-PACK: _____

12TH MUST-PACK: _____

I hope that you have come to understand how beautiful you are because of Whose you are. The God that made you is pleased with His creation. He wants us to find our worth in Him. Let's stop focusing on trying to live up to the world's beauty standards and focus on God's designs for us. When you start to feel yourself becoming burdened again with the demands of this world and seeking to conform to their standards, let God's Word envelope you and remind you of what He has to say about you. Then, be set free, transformed into a living example of His glory.

Let's take care of our bodies, God's temple, by being mindful of what we put in it and on it. I want to take care of my body and be healthy. I desire to have all of the strength and energy I need to serve my Lord. I exercise, try to eat nutritious foods and rest in order to care for my temple. However, I always keep this is mind, "For physical training is of some value, but godliness has value for all things, holding promise for both the present life and the life to come" (1 Timothy 4:8). I work to keep my focus in check. I want to invest more time and energy in the eternal rather than the temporal.

As we close, I hope that the next time you see a butterfly that you will remember what we learned about God's transforming power and that it brings a smile to your face.

PEOPLE AND PRAYER

College will undoubtedly challenge you, change you and cause you to question who you are. A great deal of the reason for all of this introspection and growth will come in the form of a walking, living, breathing human being that sleeps in the bed right next to you. That's right, I'm talking about your roommates.

You've spent the last eighteen years with a family who has grown accustomed to your quirks, preferences and routine. Now, here you are, thrown into a room the size of a prison cell and told you have to make it work with your new cellmate (Oops! I mean roommate!). Whether you went potluck and are meeting your roommate for the first time or if you're bunking up with an old friend, the challenges are the same. This person doesn't know all of your weird little habits like your family did and they may have a totally different way of doing things. For example, my family knew that I wasn't a morning person and therefore, didn't talk to me until I was awake for an hour! What if you're like me and your roommate is Susie Sunshine at 6 am? Thankfully, none of my college roommates resembled anything close to an enthusiastic early riser like dear Susie. However, we did have complications and had to make some adjustments in order to make it work.

I want to tell you about my roommate from my freshman year, Richale. She was wonderful, sweet and fun to be around and for those reasons I considered myself very blessed to have her as my roomie. Nevertheless, she was from Ohio and I was from Texas, and our upbringings had been very different. She had been to church before but we didn't view Christianity the same. I learned a great deal about myself because of Richale. One of the greatest epiphanies, or aha moments, about who I was came from her. One such aha moment came fall semester after I had come back to my dorm room from classes and was feeling really stressed. I had just been bombarded with a slew of assignments and projects and got a test grade back that I wasn't particularly proud of. I was relieved to find the room empty and remembered that Richale was still in class. I knew I just needed a little time to unwind before I began to tackle all that loomed before me. It seemed as though I had just sat down and taken a deep breath when Richale walked in. She was elated because her class had let out early and she wanted to tell me all about it. I tried to be polite and give her the "uh huh" with everything she said, hoping that she would get the hint that I didn't want to talk. I was trying to listen patiently until she was done so I could get back to my unwinding, which was really more like a pity party. After a few minutes of talking, I just couldn't handle it anymore and said, "Richale! I just really don't feel like talking right now."

My words cut her and she left the room crying. I felt worse than I had before and kicked myself for not just keeping quiet. What had I just done? Why was I being so selfish and rude? After a couple of hours, she came back to the room and was ready to talk. I told her how sorry I was and tried to explain my plight. She explained that she had been frustrated with me because she felt she never knew what she would be coming home to, happy Kate or stressed-out Kate, and she just didn't know how to handle it. She told me she felt like she had to "walk on eggshells around me." That last line stung because I remember hearing the exact phrase used about me from my mom and sister. And then, there it was. It was as if a big sign decked out in flashing lights and a pointy red arrow dropped from the sky over my head and read, "Selfish Brat!" and deep conviction set in.

After again apologizing to Richale, I called my mom and told her what happened. She tried, without much success, to muffle her laugh! She got tickled by the thought that someone else had to deal with all of my antics and that I was finally realizing what she had been putting up with for so many years. She tried to comfort me and told me that what I experienced was so much of what college and especially having roommates is about.

You see, your roommate unknowingly is holding up a mirror that helps you see yourself in a whole new way. I learned that I let my emotions get the best of me, and that when I was stressed, I undeservedly treated others badly. That fateful day, I asked the Lord's forgiveness for my selfishness and determined to change my behavior. I still struggle with not letting my circumstances affect my treatment of people. However, I've come a long way over the years and am thankful to have seen my reflection through that roommate shaped mirror.

I feel so thankful to have had that time with Richale. I appreciate her graciousness towards me as I learned and grew, and I am thankful for all of the lessons I learned. Now, I have a dear friend in Richale and I am a better roommate to my husband because of all I learned with her.

What quirky things or personality traits do you have that may make you difficult to live with?

What are you most nervous about when you think about living with roommates?

My desire is that God would be honored in your relationships with your roommates and in all of the relationships you develop in college. In order to help you find success in your relationships, I want to give you a few practical pointers for making things work and give you the mindset we must take on as we deal with people.

Some practical pointers:

Roommates

I spent my freshman year of college with Richale at Mercyhurst College in Erie, Pennsylvania. When I went home that summer, I decided to stay in College Station, where I was from, and finish school at Texas A&M University (*whoop!*). Two of my friends from high school had the same idea. Melissa had spent her freshman year at Texas Tech and Sharon had been at Lipscomb University in Tennessee. The three of us found a little rent house in College Station and convinced our parents to let us move in together. We were so excited! *Our first house!* We were starting to feel like grown-ups, or at least semi-grown up college kids. Each of us had roommates in the dorms and we were looking forward to taking the wisdom we had gleaned to make things even better this go 'round. We had a list of items we discussed and then wrote a contract that we all signed and posted on the fridge. On it, we listed a few of the most important guidelines we wanted to follow and the rest of it was full of scripture with our signatures on the bottom. How I wish I still had that contract to show you! But, I can tell you what we discussed and agreed upon.

Items we discussed:

Boys: We created a "curfew" at the house for guys. This meant that, after a certain hour, they couldn't come over. We also had an "Open Door Policy", meaning that when guys were over, we kept the doors open.

Bills: We divided up the bills and decided who would pay what bills and when they were due. In our case, Melissa handled paying the bills and Sharon and I paid her. For us, that worked out great. She would tell us each month what we owed and we paid her. I had friends that had a corkboard in the house where bills were posted and a little white board next to it. The person responsible for sending in the check would post the bill on the board and then write each person's names on the white board with the amount owed and due date. The person's name would get erased when the bill was paid. I liked that system because it helped keep everyone accountable. If you use this method, post the board somewhere out of the way. You don't want guests to snoop out your private information. The point here is that you all communicate about the bills and faithfully pay what you owe.

Chores: We made a list of the chores that needed to be done each week and then assigned them to each roommate. Our chore list was specific so that people knew exactly what to do. For example, instead of just putting "Clean the Bathroom", it would have details like: clean the toilet, bathtub, mirrors, sink and sweep the floor. Each person in our house did the same chores every week. There were certain personal chores that we each agreed to in order to keep the house neat. For example, we all agreed to take care of our own dishes and keep shared areas neat by putting things away.

Roommate Night: We wanted to make sure that we did a good job communicating with one another not just about house stuff, but also about our lives. Therefore, we had roommate night on Wednesday night every other week and ate dinner together. We took turns making meals for each other.

Food: We each bought our own food and ate only our own food! This is tricky; especially when you're all out of milk and your roomie has a full gallon just chilling in the fridge. If you decide not to share food, make sure you don't steal food, and that if it's an emergency, you ask and then promptly replace. We didn't share food because we had heard of too many sticky situations that arose from friends that had. Therefore, we decided to steer clear of such conflicts. Each of us had our own shelves in the kitchen and our own shelves in the fridge where we kept our food.

Clothes/Things: We agreed that if we borrowed someone's clothes or things that we would return them as good as or better than we found them. It doesn't matter if you're borrowing a book, a blow-dryer, a shirt, shoes or a belt; you should aim to take care of it like it was your own, or better. If in borrowing, you damage or destroy something of your roommates, you should offer to replace or fix the item. We agreed to ALWAYS ask before borrowing. If the roommate wasn't around and we couldn't reach her, we didn't borrow it because we didn't have approval. When you ask, pay attention to your roommate's response. If you ask her and she hesitates, you might reconsider borrowing the item. You don't want to run the risk of borrowing something precious to her that could get ruined or damaged.

Schedules: We discussed schedules and routines in order to be respectful of each other's need for quiet so that we could sleep and study. This pointer is especially crucial if you share a dorm room or a room together in a house. Talk with your roommate(s) about their schedule. When are their classes? When do they usually get up and go to bed? When will they need to have quiet in the room? I remember with Richale, that if either of us came home and the other was napping or doing some intense studying, we would get what we needed and go hang out someplace else for a while.

I recommend that you take the time to talk to your roommates about boys, bills, chores, food, a possible roommate night, clothes and schedules. You can use the guidelines that we followed or create new ones that work better for your situation. Whether you're in a dorm room or a house, these pointers can be tailored to help you. Clear communication about expectations will help prevent resentment and conflict. If you agree that a contract would help seal the deal, then create one. We had a good time finding scripture for ours and putting it together. We decorated it with cute fonts, designs and colors.

As I mentioned, the contract wasn't necessarily a long list of rules. What we hung on the fridge was really a compilation of scripture; verses like: "As for me and my household, we will serve the Lord" (Joshua 24:15b) and "Be kind and compassionate to one another, forgiving each other, just as in Christ God forgave you" (Ephesians 4:32). We knew that these verses really got to the heart of the matter and would influence our decisions more than a list of rules. We prayed over it before we signed it. We also took the time to pray over our house and the time we would spend there.

Melissa's father came over and led us in a prayer on moving day. He asked the Lord to keep us safe from harm and to use our little house to give Him big glory. I loved our little Jane house; named for its location at 409 Jane Street. It may have been small but it was full of warmth and blessed memories. We had so much fun there. We laughed together, cried together, hosted Bible studies, entertained friends, curled up on the couch to watch movies, studied and grew so much. It was in that house, knelt on the living room floor, that my dear friends put their hands on me and prayed for me when I re-connected with Jeremy and realized my love for him.

Don't get me wrong. We had our disagreements and spats. However, because of our shared love for the Lord and the planning we had done to help things run smoothly, we always got back on track. I want you to know what we did that worked at the Jane House so that you can prepare ahead of time for lessons we learned only through hindsight.

Friends

Why a section on roommates and then a note about friends? Aren't they the same thing? Well… yes and no. There is a distinction. Your roommates may not necessarily be your friends and that's okay. I want to make this clear because I think that too many gals head off to college thinking that their roommate is going to be their best buddy. Even if you go to college with your best friend from high school, they may not stay that way while you're there. I'm sorry if this makes you a little sad, but it's true and I want to prepare you ahead of time for what may otherwise be a rude awakening. The fact is that people change in college and may not be like they were when they first arrived.

Please keep your roommates' feelings in mind as you bring friends in and out. First, if you know that your roommate does not like one of your friends, try and be respectful of her feelings. When you share a dorm room, there is not a lot of room for your roommate to remove herself from that person. If you want to hang out with them, go to a common area or another friend's place. Second, if you are aware that you're roommate is having a hard time meeting people and seems lonely, try and make them feel welcome where you are. I know this can be difficult and I'm not saying that she needs to become your BFF. Just let her know that she is welcome.

The most important pointer about friends in college: make sure that your best friends, your closest friends, are believers. You want to surround yourself with people that are going to help you make God-honoring decisions and hold you accountable. Remember that you are going to be facing all kinds of new challenges and you need the people that are closest to you to help you make good choices. 1 Corinthians 15:33 warns us, "Bad company corrupts good character."

Parents

Your relationship with your parents will be affected most by your move to college. You will leave their nest and figure out how to fly on your own. Think for a moment about how difficult this must be on the people that have raised you. To them, it feels like just yesterday that they brought a newborn baby home to care for and now, as if in a flash, you're ready to leave home. I don't want you to feel guilty or sad. I want you to keep their feelings in mind and remember to honor what they have done for you by raising you. Ephesians 6:1-3 says, "Children, obey your parents in the Lord, for this is right "Honor your father and mother"—which is the first commandment with a promise—"that it may go well with you and that you may enjoy long life on the earth."

We honor them, in part, by letting them know how we are doing and by telling them how much we love them and how thankful we are for them. Practically, this means that we give them a call, send them an email or write them a note.

Another way we honor what they have done for us is by giving our best at school and in our studies. Your parents have invested so much in you. They have clothed you, fed you, nurtured and taught you. We need to honor that upbringing. Try to put yourself in their position. How would you want them to behave? Write your response in the space below:

You'd probably want your child to go to class instead of skipping, take notes, study, take care of themselves and call home regularly! Someday, you will realize what a big deal it was that your parents raised and provided for you. You don't want to look back and regret the way you treated their gift.

I wanted to give you some practical pointers for your relationships with your roommates, friends and parents. Do you remember them? Write a practical pointer under each topic that you will use:

Roommates:

Friends:

Parents:

Those practical pointers are going to be a big help. However, you could follow every rule and guideline and still run into trouble in your relationships. What we have to keep in check is the attitude of our hearts toward others. Are we only looking out for ourselves? Do we follow the rules but do so with a resentful attitude? We have to do a heart check. Not against the hearts of those around us but against the heart of the Only One we seek to imitate. You see, true success in our relationships comes from our imitation of Christ. We want to take on His attitude. What was His attitude?

Read the following passage and keep an eye out for the way Christ's attitude is described.

> If you have any encouragement from being united with Christ, if any comfort from his love, if any fellowship with the Spirit, if any tenderness and compassion, then make my joy complete by being like-minded, having the same love, being one in spirit and purpose. Do nothing out of selfish ambition or vain conceit, but in humility consider others better than yourselves. Each of you should look not only to your own interests, but also to the interests of others.

> Your attitude should be the same as that of Christ Jesus:
> Who, being in very nature God,
>   did not consider equality with God something to be grasped,
>   but made himself nothing,
>   **taking the very nature of a servant,**
>   being made in human likeness.
> And being found in appearance as a man,
>   he humbled himself
>   and became obedient to death—
>   even death on a cross!
> Therefore God exalted him to the highest place
>   and gave him the name that is above every name,
> that at the name of Jesus every knee should bow,
>   in heaven and on earth and under the earth,
>   and every tongue confess that Jesus Christ is Lord,
>   to the glory of God the Father (Philippians 2:1-11, emphasis mine).

I hope that you saw it there. Look back at the verse if you need to and fill in the blank:

Taking the very nature of a _____.

This is Jesus Christ we're talking about here. He is the King of Kings and Lord of Lords but He didn't feel the need to put a crown on His head and sit on a throne. No, He took the opposite approach. He humbled Himself to the lowest position and became a servant. We want to follow the example of Christ. Therefore, we have to add the next must-pack to our college-bound suitcase.

13TH MUST-PACK: BE A SERVANT

Christ's most amazing act of servitude came when He laid down His life for you and me. Before that monumental day, He lived out a servant's heart in His life. An incredible example of this came when Christ washed the feet of His disciples. We find an account of this act in John 13:1-17:

> It was just before the Passover Feast. Jesus knew that the time had come for him to leave this world and go to the Father. Having loved his own who were in the world, he now showed them the full extent of his love.
>
> The evening meal was being served, and the devil had already prompted Judas Iscariot, son of Simon, to betray Jesus. Jesus knew that the Father had put all things under his power, and that he had come from God and was returning to God; so he got up from the meal, took off his outer clothing, and wrapped a towel around his waist. After that, he poured water into a basin and began to wash his disciples' feet, drying them with the towel that was wrapped around him.
>
> He came to Simon Peter, who said to him, "Lord, are you going to wash my feet?"
>
> Jesus replied, "You do not realize now what I am doing, but later you will understand."
>
> "No," said Peter, "you shall never wash my feet."
>
> Jesus answered, "Unless I wash you, you have no part with me."
>
> "Then, Lord," Simon Peter replied, "not just my feet but my hands and my head as well!"
>
> Jesus answered, "A person who has had a bath needs only to wash his feet; his whole body is clean. And you are clean, though not every one of you." For he knew who was going to betray him, and that was why he said not every one was clean.
>
> When he had finished washing their feet, he put on his clothes and returned to his place. "Do you understand what I have done for you?" he asked them. You call me 'Teacher' and 'Lord,' and rightly so, for that is what I am. *Now that I, your Lord and Teacher, have washed your feet, you also should wash one another's feet. I have set you an example that you should do as I have done for you.* I tell you the truth, no servant is greater than his master, nor is a messenger greater than the one who sent him. Now that you know these things, you will be blessed if you do them (emphasis mine).

Christ was providing the disciples with an object lesson that had several implications for them. Don't you love it when your teachers use objects that you can see and interact with to help you get the lesson? I am completely visual and "get it" so much more when I can see it. This lesson comes just before Christ's death and He knew it was time for the disciples to really "get it!" He pulled out all the stops and gave them a clear object lesson in which He physically showed them what He was metaphorically expecting of them.

So what was the lesson? The washing has a two-fold application. The New Testament Explorer explains, "By washing the feet of the disciples Jesus demonstrated **humility and service**, and also taught the need for **daily cleansing** of His followers in order for them to be effectively used in such service" (Mark Bailey and Tom Constable, p. 183, empahasis mine).

What were the two reasons for the cleansing?

1. Jesus demonstrated _____ and _____

2. The need for _____ _____ of His followers

The cleansing is crucial, and I am so eternally thankful that I have been washed clean by my Savior, but we are going to focus on the other reason Christ used the washing demonstration. I want us to see what He was trying to teach His followers, us, about service. The Bible Knowledge Commentary tells us:

> Foot-washing was needed in Palestine. The streets were dusty and people wore sandals without socks or stockings. It was a mark of honor for a host to provide a servant to wash a guest's feet; it was a breach of hospitality not to provide for it. Wives often washed their husbands' feet, and children washed their parents' feet. Most people, of course, had to wash their own feet.

Why was foot-washing necessary in Jesus' day?

Is it necessary in our time? Why not?

What are some practical ways we take care of our guests in modern times?

Shoes and paved roads make it no longer necessary for us to wash the feet of our guests. Can I get a hallelujah? However, there are other things we do for them when they enter our homes. I was taught to take the coat, packages and suitcases from visitors and offer them a place to sit and something to drink. This seems mild, however, compared to what was involved in washing someone's feet. Picture it. Feet, and not the regularly pedicured kind, covered in dirt and parked on the floor a foot from your face and you have to wash them. Could you do it? Taking someone's coat and offering them water is pretty easy and makes me look like a nice, well-mannered person. But what if I had to get down on the floor and scrub some dusty, sweaty, calloused feet? Not so appealing or easy to do. Yet my Jesus did it, and He did it for a reason. The Bible Knowledge Commentary explains that Jesus was teaching them that, "Meeting others' needs self-sacrificially is what they ought to do too." Christ put his own needs and position aside and took the role of a servant in order to care for His disciples. Jesus demonstrated for us how to meet others needs sacrificially. The first reason we serve is because **He served**.

As we discussed, foot washing isn't really necessary in our culture. But, think about this. If Jesus were a student on your campus, how do you think He would behave? He may not walk around with a towel carrying a wash basin, but what might He do?

Picture Jesus, let's call Him J.C., walking around on your campus disguised as a college student and answer these questions:

How would he act?

How would he treat others?

Where would He spend His time?

Would He go to class?

Would He fight with the teacher?

Would He do His work?

How awesome it would be to go to college with Christ and see His life lived out! I imagine that He would be well liked except by those He made feel threatened. I imagine that He would be the first one to take you to class if your car broke down, the first one to carry your books, the first one to offer a listening ear and the first one to pray with you and present your requests to His Father. I also imagine that He would give His best in His classes. I think that His willingness to live out a servant's attitude would spill over into his homework, attention and attendance in class. We want to serve on our campuses because He would have. Our service is not a "have to" thing. It is a willingness to put yourself and your status aside in order to meet the needs of another.

Keep in mind that we are following the example of Jesus, the Son of God, who is now seated on His throne at the right hand of the Father. The man with the highest position and greatest authority did not need to set Himself up on a throne while here on this Earth. Instead, He wrapped a towel around his waist and put His knees on dusty ground in order to serve. Jesus knew who He was. It didn't get in the way of His serving; it actually freed Him up to serve. The New Testament Explorer describes explains how this mindset applies to believers, "Security in one's position in Christ gives freedom to serve others in genuine humility" (Mark Bailey and Tom Constable, p. 183).

Jesus is teaching us here that we imitate Him best not by setting ourselves up on a throne, but by getting on our knees. Sometimes it is easy to serve, and I feel so blessed to do it. Other times it's hard—like when I know I may not receive recognition for my acts of kindness, believe they are beneath me or may make me look bad.

> Lorne Sanny, the founder of Navigators, was once asked how you could tell if you were really a servant. "By how you act," he said, "when you're treated like one" (*Your God is Too Safe*, Mark Buchanan, p. 212).

Our ability to serve is rooted in our security in Christ. When we feel secure with who we are in Him, we feel free to serve no matter how nasty the job. However, when we struggle with insecurity, we usually react one of two ways. We either build ourselves up in front of others or we allow others to walk all over us. Often, we want to serve when it makes us look good. "If it makes me look better to others, I'm all for it" but when it may actually make you look like a servant, it becomes pretty hard to get off of that high horse and down to your knees. I've allowed my insecurity to swing this direction. I remember walking into college mixers and feeling overwhelmed with all of the new people in the room. My immediate goal would be to get all of them to like me and think I was something special. I would go on and on about myself to make sure that they were impressed. I wasn't looking out for the needs of anyone but myself. If someone needed something from me in that moment, I was oblivious.

On the other end of the spectrum, my insecurity has dropped me to the doormat position. I have sought security in others and their recognition of me as a sweet girl. Again, I wanted everyone to like me, and I never wanted to hurt anyone's feeling. Therefore, I allowed others to treat me badly. I wasn't able to say "no" to relationships that caused me deep heartache and deterred me from following God's plan.

Where do you fall on the scale? Does your insecurity have you in the doormat position? Does it cause you to build yourself up in front of others so that you sit high above everyone in the throne position? Or with your security resting confidently in Christ, do you find yourself on your knees ready to serve? Circle where you most often fall on this scale:

Desperate   **Serving in**   **Boastfully**
Doormat   **Security**   **Built-Up**

I have been all over this scale. What I have learned to remember is that I find all that I need in Christ. All of my confidence, all of my security and all of my worth come from Him. Therefore, I don't have to worry about getting ahead or trying to make myself look good. I have a Jesus that loves me completely, and therefore, I serve. This is the second reason we serve: we find our worth in Christ and serve because **we are secure in Him**. Because I know who I am and who I would have been without His love, I serve my God by serving others.

There is another reason that we serve. This little anecdote may help you figure it out:

> There is a Hassidic legend about a community of Jewish monks that had descended into factionalism, rivalry, gossip, suspicion. A wise man visited the abbey, and the abbot told him about the deplorable condition of the monks. "It is so bad," he said, "that I do not believe we will survive as a community."
>
> "I am so surprised," the other man said. "For it is widely rumored the Messiah is in your midst."
>
> The abbot went back and reported to the monks the conversation. It entirely transformed the place. Each treated all the others with deep love and high regard—this one might be the Messiah (Mark Buchanan, *Your God is Too Safe*, p. 215, emphasis mine).

Their attitudes completely changed because they believed the Messiah was among them. How would our attitudes change if we believed we might be serving Jesus? Hmm... let's take a look at Matthew 25:34-40:

> Then the King will say to those on his right, 'Come, you who are blessed by my Father; take your inheritance, the kingdom prepared for you since the creation of the world. For I was hungry and you gave me something to eat, I was thirsty and you gave me something to drink, I was a stranger and you invited me in, I needed clothes and you clothed me, I was sick and you looked after me, I was in prison and you came to visit me.'

Then the righteous will answer him, 'Lord, when did we see you hungry and feed you, or thirsty and give you something to drink? When did we see you a stranger and invite you in, or needing clothes and clothe you? When did we see you sick or in prison and go to visit you?'

The King will reply, 'I tell you the truth, whatever you did for one of the least of these brothers of mine, you did for me.'

The Jewish monks wondered if they might encounter the Messiah in their service. Matthew 25 told us that we do encounter Him in our service. When I serve others, I am serving Christ. Oh, I pray for eyes to see each person as a though they were my Jesus. How differently would I treat them! How quickly would I rush to serve them!

How do you think you would treat people differently if you knew that they could be Jesus?

May we take on the attitude of the Jewish monks. Ladies, the Messiah is in our midst! As we serve "the least of these," we are serving Him. This is the third reason we serve: by doing so, **we are serving Him.**

We follow the must-pack to Be a Servant for three reasons. I underlined them above. Please fill in the blanks: *Because...*

    1. He _____

    2. We are _____ ____ _____

    3. We are _____ _____

We discussed the Greatest Commandment in the Time Management chapter. If you recall, we found it in Mark 12:30-31, "Love the Lord your God with all your heart and with all your soul and with all your mind and with all your strength. The second is this: 'Love your neighbor as yourself. There is no commandment greater than these."

Based on this scripture, please put these people in order. Here are your options: Others, You, Jesus

Who comes 1st:_____

Who is 2nd:_____

Who becomes 3rd:_____

I have heard this concept explained as an acrostic using the word JOY. We find joy in following God's command to live life in order with Jesus first, Others second and You last. Our culture teaches that life is all about you. They say that you need to "get yours" and not worry about who you step on to get there. In comparison to the Greatest Commandment, God is calling us to take on the opposite attitude.

Putting yourself third in order to serve others is not always easy. Why is it hard for you to serve?

Keeping the mindset of a servant, though difficult at times, will help you as you approach every relationship. When you put others before yourself you will find that you have fewer quarrels, that fights are settled quickly and that the people you interact with are helped and encouraged.

When we have a servant mindset, we are concerned about the needs of others. The greatest need you will find on your college campus is a lost soul's need for Christ.

14TH MUST-PACK: YOUR CAMPUS IS YOUR MISSION FIELD

"Mission field?" you ask, "I'm not sure I've been called to missions." The answer: You have. Many people wait for a "call" to missions before they go and serve; they've confused international missions with living on mission no matter where you are.

Jesus calls us to live on mission. What is our mission? It was given to us in the Great Commission: "Therefore go and make disciples of all nations, baptizing them in the name of the Father and of the Son and of the Holy Spirit, and teaching them to obey everything I have commanded you" (Matthew 28:19-20). The scripture doesn't say, "Therefore go abroad..." No, it just says "go"! We are here to make Christ followers of all people. We have to live with a mission mentality; it is our calling.

2 Corinthians 5:20a solidifies this truth, "We are therefore Christ's ambassadors, as though God were making his appeal through us." We, means you and I and ambassador is defined by Dictionary.com as, "an authorized messenger or representative." The position has two main roles: to accurately represent the Messenger and to bring a message. As representatives, we must **live it**, and as messengers we must **tell it**.

We are to live as Christ's ambassadors, on a mission for the kingdom. How do we do it? How do we live our lives as ambassadors on a mission? Do we stand on the corner and pass out gospel tracks or hop up on a platform in our campus courtyard and preach? That approach may be necessary at times but our culture is pretty jaded by Christians who preach about Jesus but don't reflect Him in the way they live. Brennan Manning, author of *The Ragamuffin Gospel*, said, "The greatest single cause of atheism in the world today are Christians who acknowledge Jesus with their lips and walk out the door and deny Him by their lifestyle. That is what an unbelieving world simply finds unbelievable."

As ambassadors, we fulfill the first part of our mission by the way we represent Christ, which means we have to live it. Have you ever heard the expression, "If you're going to talk the talk, you better walk the walk"? We need to live out the gospel message of Jesus. People don't want to hear us talk until they've seen our walk. St. Francis of Assisi is believed to have said, "Preach Christ at all times and, if necessary, use words."

We have to live out Jesus in our lives. We do that by pursuing holiness, serving others and by building relationships with people. We preach Christ to them first, with our "walk"—the way we live. As we get to know non-believers, conversations will open up. They will notice that you are different and their hearts will be ready. Then, by divine appointment, the Holy Spirit will prepare you and give you the words to say, and they will fall on fertile soil. That's when, as Christ's messenger, you tell it.

Don't fall under the lie that living it is enough. Your lifestyle will open the door, but your words will tell the rest of the story. As ambassadors, we represent Christ and bring His message.

Why is it hard for you to preach Christ by the way you live?

Why is it hard for you to tell others about Jesus?

Be careful that you don't get so caught up in your own little world that you forget that your lecture hall, dorm building and campus are full of people that don't know Jesus. Don't surrender to the lie that college is all about you and what you can achieve. Please understand that your success glorifies the Lord, but He has a larger purpose for you being at college. In everything you do, going to class, doing your work, eating lunch, hanging out with friends, preach Christ by your actions. Then, when you have opportunity, preach Christ by your words. Live it AND tell it! Because, after all, aren't you thankful that someone told you?

I heard the song, "Up to Me", for the first time when I was in high school. The author, Ross King, was a college student who led worship for Breakaway, a ministry at Texas A&M. I wanted to share it with you because I believe it summarizes our mission.

Me and my friends, we've got the social thing down pat
Look for us on Friday night, you'll always find us there
They know I'm a Christian; they've got no problems with that
And sometimes I don't even drink and no one seems to care
But we don't ever have deep conversations, so I never get a chance to share my heart

You know someone outta tell them about Jesus
They need to know, they need to see
Someone outta tell them about Jesus
But that's just not my gift so you probably shouldn't leave that up to me

I am a leader almost everywhere I go, honors and positions cover my identity
I have good morals and sure everybody knows,
That God and church and family are important things to me
I know there are people who need Jesus all around, but I'm sure my actions speak for me

You know someone outta tell them about Jesus
They need to know, they need to see
Someone outta tell them about Jesus
But that's just not my gift so you probably shouldn't leave that up to me

I sang my song for a thousand just last night
I sang of Jesus' love and I made sure that I was heard
But in my class today to my left and to my right
Two lost souls were falling fast and I didn't say a word

You know someone outta tell them about Jesus
They need to know, they need to see
Someone outta tell them about Jesus
But that's just not my gift so you probably shouldn't leave that up to me

Ross was convicted. He knew that he was being called to reflect Christ in his lifestyle but that it didn't stop there. There were people in his classes that he knew didn't know Jesus and he needed to tell them. He tried to give the excuse that he wasn't gifted with evangelism, but the sarcasm in his lyrics reveals that he knew better. He knew that it really was up to him and he needed to "tell them about Jesus."

We must live on mission on our campuses. Our mission is to bring others to the saving knowledge of Jesus Christ. We fulfill that mission by first living it, and secondly, by telling it.
Which part of our mission is hardest for you, living it or telling it? Why?

Our mission isn't easy, but I want you to know that God has given you everything you need to accomplish your calling. He never gives us an end without providing the means. I pray that you have many opportunities to share your faith on your college campus in your lifestyle and through your testimony. I echo the prayer of Paul in Philemon for you, "I pray that you may be active in sharing your faith, so that you will have a full understanding of every good thing we have in Christ." (Philemon 1:6) We reap an amazing blessing when we are present for the acceptance of a new soul into heaven. We gain a more complete understanding of "every good thing we have in Christ"—His grace, His kindness, His mercy and His love.

Remember, our mission is two-fold:
        We are representatives, which means we _____ it and
        We are messengers, which means we _____ it.

Let's live on mission; as Christ's representatives and messengers, "as though God were making His appeal through us" (2 Corinthians 5:20a).

Can you believe that we are about to put the final must-pack into our college suitcase? We've talked about anxiety, the testing of our faith, finding a church, how to manage our time, guys, dating, taking care of our bodies, roommates, witnessing…Did I miss anything? We've covered a lot. With all of the issues we've discussed in mind, we are ready to add the 15th must-pack:

15TH **MUST-PACK:**
PRAY IN EVERY CIRCUMSTANCE

You are about to embark on an adventure to a whole new world. Although it seems like everything is about to change, one thing will remain: God is with you. He is consistent and reliable. He wants to be Your Guide through the wild ride. Remember, He will never leave you or forsake you (Hebrews 13:5). He will be with you through it all and wants to talk with you through every part. He wants to hear about it when you meet an amazing new friend or make an awesome grade on a paper. He wants to talk to you when you're feeling lonely and missing home. He wants to talk to you when you feel stressed and ready to crack.

On this new adventure, you will encounter amazing triumphs, tough trials and make-you-wanna-quit moments. In all of these, go to the Lord in prayer.

I have given you three scriptures concerning prayer. As you read each of them, please do two things: First, circle the word PRAY, PRAYER, PRAYING. Second, underline ALL, ALWAYS, EVERYTHING, CONTINUALLY.

> And pray in the Spirit on all occasions with all kinds of prayers and requests. With this in mind, be alert and always keep on praying for all the saints (Ephesians 6:18).

> Do not be anxious about anything, but in everything, by prayer and petition, with thanksgiving, present your requests to God. And the peace of God, which transcends all understanding, will guard your hearts and your minds in Christ Jesus (Philippians 4:6-7).

> Be joyful always; pray continually; give thanks in all circumstances, for this is God's will for you in Christ Jesus (1 Thessalonians 5:16-18).

What are these scriptures saying? **PRAY IN EVERY CIRCUMSTANCE**

No matter what is going on with you: PRAY! Think about your prayer life like your cell phone plan. Did you sign up for one of those plans where you get 10 minutes a month and therefore only use your phone in emergencies? Or do you have the unlimited plan? You talk so much that you need a blue tooth in your ear so you can just chat away all day long. I want to live out my prayer life on the unlimited plan—a hands-free, constant connection to the God of the Universe. The Lord is calling us to the unlimited plan. He desires a constant connection with you. Whatever you're doing, wherever you're going, He wants to talk to you. So much so, that He built you with your very own hands free device, the Holy Spirit. The Spirit is with you constantly and you are always dialed in. If you've been living on the, "In case of emergency plan," SWITCH! Contact your Provider and tell Him you are ready for an upgrade. Sister, college will be a whirlwind like you have not yet known. You want that constant lifeline as you face each new hardship and hallelujah moment.

In all of our circumstances, we must pray. For each circumstance we may encounter, God has told us how to respond:

What should I do when I don't know what God has planned for me?
> 'For I know the plans I have for you,' declares the LORD, 'plans to prosper you and not to harm you, plans to give you hope and a future. Then you will call upon me and come and pray to me, and I will listen to you. You will seek me and find me when you seek me with all your heart' (Jeremiah 29:11-13).

What should I do when people are being mean to me and I just want to retaliate?
> But I tell you: Love your enemies and pray for those who persecute you (Matthew 5:44).

What should I do when I am tempted to sin?
> Pray that you will not fall into temptation (Luke 22:40b).

What should I do when I'm in trouble?
> Is any one of you in trouble? He should pray (James 5:13).

What should I do when I'm happy and thankful?
> Is anyone happy? Let him sing songs of praise (James 5:13).

What should I do when I know I have sinned and need forgiveness?

> And the prayer offered in faith will make the sick person well; the Lord will raise him up. If he has sinned, he will be forgiven. Therefore confess your sins to each other and pray for each other so that you may be healed. The prayer of a righteous man is powerful and effective (James 5:15-16).

I see my prayer life as a continual conversation with the Lord and I don't find any incident too small to take to Him. He is concerned with every aspect of your life and cares deeply for you. He wants to talk with you about your day, your struggles, your needs and the good things that He's doing for you. It's amazing the change that comes about when we pray. The Message paraphrases Philippians 4:6-7 this way: "Don't fret or worry. Instead of worrying, pray. Let petitions and praises shape your worries into prayers, letting God know your concerns. Before you know it, a sense of God's wholeness, everything coming together for good, will come and settle you down. It's wonderful what happens when Christ displaces worry at the center of your life." I need a little settling down when I get worked up, and I am thankful for the constant connection I have with my Father who offers me help as soon as I call on Him.

Please take a moment to put this must-pack into practice. Write a prayer to the Lord in the space below. You might: Thank Him for all that He has done and is doing for you. Try to be specific. Tell Him about the things that are troubling or worrying you.

I encourage you to keep a prayer journal. The Lord helps me sort out my craziness through pages of prayers. When I look back at my entries, I see how my prayer started out with worry and stress. Then, truly, the peace of God would flow into my mind and through the ink and I would see the worry worked out. My prayer journals help me to be mindful of what I've requested and thanked God for, so that my eyes are opened to the way He works things out. Don't miss the blessing. After you present it, watch for Him to do His work.

Romans 12:9-16 perfectly summarizes our three must-packs from this chapter. We learned to serve, live it, tell it and pray. Next to each line from this verse, write the most appropriate action based on what we discussed; you might even need to write two. I've done the first one for you:

SERVE, LIVE IT, TELL IT OR *PRAY*

Love must be sincere. SERVE & LIVE IT

Hate what is evil; cling to what is good. _____

Be devoted to one another in brotherly love. _____

Honor one another above yourselves. _____

Never be lacking in zeal, but keep your spiritual fervor, serving the Lord. _____

Be joyful in hope, _____

patient in affliction, _____

faithful in prayer. _____

Share with God's people who are in need. _____

Practice hospitality. _____

Bless those who persecute you; bless and do not curse. _____

Rejoice with those who rejoice; mourn with those who mourn. _____

Live in harmony with one another. _____

Do not be proud, but be willing to associate with people of low position. _____

Do not be conceited. _____

God wants to use you on your campus. He is sending you out on a mission. Remember to serve others. Remember to reflect Christ in your lifestyle. Remember to tell others about His goodness. Call to Him for help, strength, wisdom and endurance to accomplish your task.

We packed the final three must-packs in this chapter. Do you remember them?

13TH MUST-PACK:_____

14TH MUST-PACK:_____

15TH MUST-PACK:_____

I am so proud of all of your hard work and believe that God will bless your desire to follow hard after Him in your college years. I am praying for you as you embark on this journey and asking God to hold you so close to Himself that you can hear Him guiding you every step of the way.

MUST
PACK
LIST

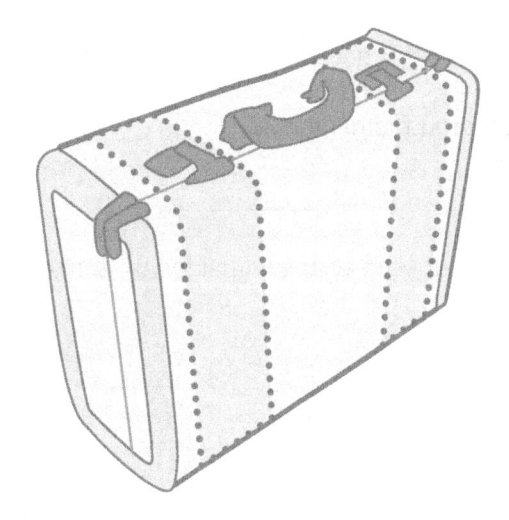
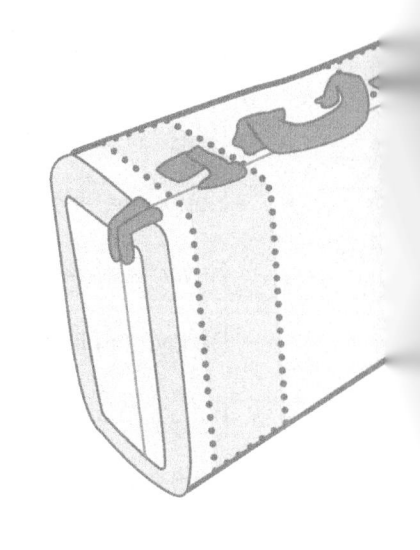

1. ## SEEK GOD FIRST
   But seek first His kingdom and His righteousness, and all these things will be given to you as well. Matthew 6:33

2. ## SPEND TIME WITH THE LORD
   I seek You with all my heart; do not let me stray from Your commands. Psalm 119:10

3. ## GET PLUGGED INTO A LOCAL CHURCH
   Now you are the body of Christ, and each one of you is a part of it. 1 Corinthians 12:27

4. ## BE EFFECTIVE BY BEING SELECTIVE
   I do not run like a man running aimlessly; I do not fight like a man beating the air. 1 Corinthians 9:26

5. ## REST
   Come to me, all you who are weary and burdened, and I will give you rest. Matthew 11:28

6. ## SCHEDULE YOUR TIME
   My times are in Your hands. Psalm 31:15

7. ## PURSUE EXCELLENCE TO THE END
   Whatever you do, work at it with all your heart, as working for the Lord, not for men. Colossians 3:23

8. ## GUARD YOUR HEART
   And the peace of God…will guard your hearts and your minds in Christ Jesus. Philippians 4:7

9. ## EVERY DATE IS A POTENTIAL MATE
   Do not be bound together with unbelievers… 2 Corinthians 6:14

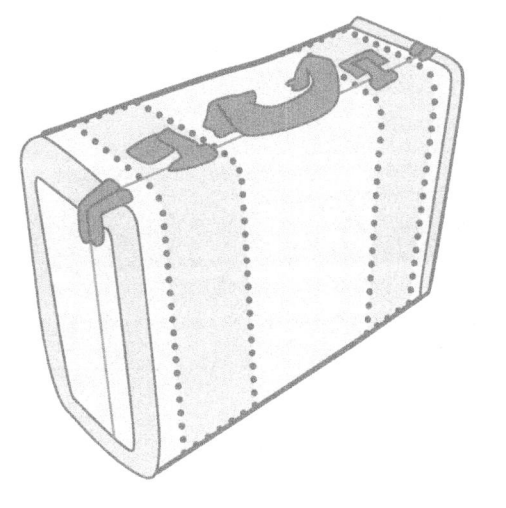
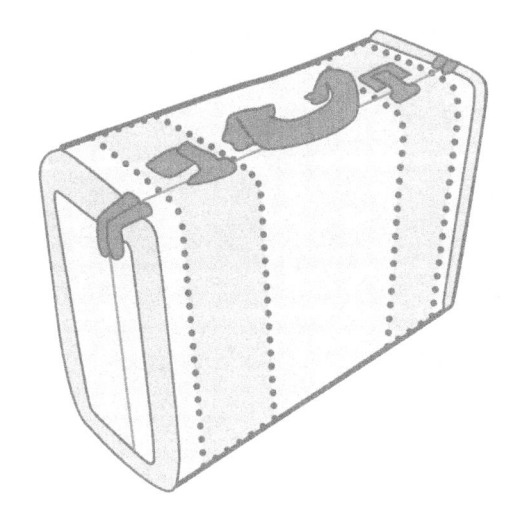
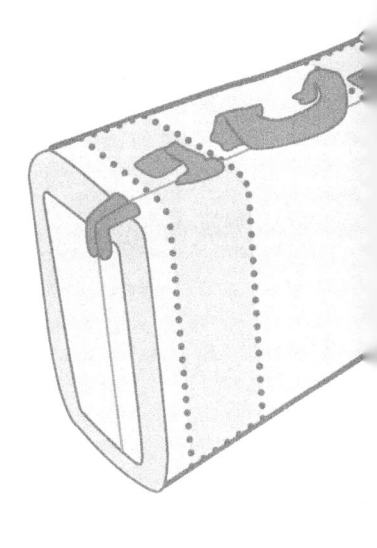

10. **PROTECT YOUR PURITY**
…for God's temple is sacred, and you are that temple. 1 Corinthians 3:16

11. **DO NOT CONFORM; BE TRANSFORMED**
Do not conform any longer to the pattern of this world, but be transformed by the renewing of your mind. Romans 12:2

12. **HONOR GOD WITH YOUR BODY** (by what you put in it and on it)
You are not your own; you were bought at a price. Therefore honor God with your body. 1 Corinthians 6:19-20

13. **BE A SERVANT**
Each of you should look not only to your own interests, but also to the interests of others. Philippians 2:4

14. **YOUR CAMPUS IS YOUR MISSION FIELD**
We are therefore Christ's ambassadors, as though God were making his appeal through us. 2 Corinthians 5:20

15. **PRAY IN EVERY CIRCUMSTANCE**
And pray in the Spirit on all occasions with all kinds of prayers and requests. Ephesians 6:18

We sure have packed a lot into one suitcase. This might be one of those times where we have to sit on top of it to get it to close! I believe it's worth the trouble, because each of these must-packs will help you significantly. Don't stuff the suitcase under the bed once you get there! Open it up and put these to use. From a girl who's been there: you'll be glad you did.

All my love,

Kate

For information on The Freshman 15 Bible Study and retreat,
go to: www.thefreshman15biblestudy.com

For copies of the Bible study or to book a retreat, contact:
Kate Henderson at kate@thefreshman15biblestudy.com

Made in the USA
Monee, IL
15 June 2020